Danielle Ross Walls is mum to two energetic and beautiful boys. In 2015, she created and directed the first careers expo for working mothers in Melbourne, the *Career Ideas for Mums Expo*. Danielle also loves freelance travel writing with an aim to get people, especially children, engaged in nature, history and conservation.

Louise Correcha is mum to a lively young daughter. She co-founded the language and writing businesses Red English and Hummingbird Writing. A former teacher, Louise now edits, writes and consults on written communication strategies for a range of technical, corporate and not-for-profit clients.

Sisters: talk to each other, be connected and informed, form women's circles, share your stories, work together, and take risks.
　Together we are invincible.

– Isabel Allende

Copyright © 2020 Danielle Ross Walls & Louise Correcha

ISBN: 978-1-922409-11-9
Published by Vivid Publishing
A division of Fontaine Publishing Group
P.O. Box 948, Fremantle
Western Australia 6959
www.vividpublishing.com.au

 A catalogue record for this book is available from the National Library of Australia

Cover design by Jo Hunt
Cover image by Blick Creative

The quote by Elizabeth Gilbert is from Oprah's SuperSoul Sunday series, season 1, episode 106.

First published in 2018 in Australia and New Zealand by Finch Publishing Pty Ltd. All rights reserved. No part of this publication may be reproduced, stored in a retrieval system or transmitted in any form or by any means, electronic, mechanical, photocopying, recording or otherwise, without the prior written permission of the copyright holder.

Working Mums

Stories by mums on how they manage children, work and life

Danielle Ross Walls
& Louise Correcha

Contents

Preface	1
Introduction	2
1. George	5
Creating Australia's first all-female rideshare service	
2. Simone	11
Mad Men to feminist: from advertising to job-share advocate	
3. Olivia	19
From high-school dropout to Cambridge scholar	
4. Mel	28
From actor to creating play-based workshops for children	
5. Rhiannon	34
A reality check, wellbeing, and the value of motherhood	
6. Jenny	43
Environmental activism, community and family life	
7. Jade	48
A corporate refugee	
8. Alisa	56
Sport, business and life	
9. Kristy	68
The Imperfect Mum community	
10. Missy	74
Motherhood, making music and a changing world	

11. Christine — 79
   The value of volunteering in creating opportunities

12. Annie — 86
   Blogging and wearing a suit for a bully-free Brownlow

13. Maria — 97
   Building a business as a sole parent with a baby

14. Danielle — 104
   Obstacles, career changes and brave ideas

15. Tiffany — 114
   Identity, work and faith

16. Aleisha — 122
   Taking the leap: starting a clinic from home

17. Chloe — 129
   Early childcare educator challenges senator on social media

18. Irene — 139
   Twenty lessons about business and life from an entrepreneur

19. Shari and Lana — 146
   Sister support

20. Jen — 153
   Building a village and a business on the other side of the world

21. Jade — 161
   Heart-centred entrepreneur travelling the world

22. Louise *Freelance writing and editing*	169
23. Carly and Alee *IVF, family and finances*	181
24. Jessica *Re-skilling and re-entering the workforce*	188
25. Amanda *Personal boundaries as a working mum*	196
26. Ella *Making a difference and running for parliament*	205
27. Kate *Taking a breath between the busyness*	212
What we wish we could have also covered	221
Finding out more	222
Helpful resources	226
Acknowledgements	230

This book is dedicated to my beautiful Nan.

– Danielle

This book is dedicated to my Czech *Maminka*, Lenka Svobodová.

– Louise

Preface

I first met Danielle when she was planning the Career Ideas for Mums Expo and she invited me to participate. Our business meeting was in the park with our young kids in tow – flexible working at its best. We immediately connected over a shared passion to support working parents and an unwavering commitment to promote family-friendly and flexible work policies.

Although *Working Mums* is about mums, the message is an all-inclusive one. It is a valuable book for dads, partners, carers, and non-parents, too.

As well as helping mums feel less alone in their struggles, *Working Mums* will also hopefully continue to fuel the flexibility conversation and help us move closer toward a situation where flexible working is the norm, rather than the exception.

Rachel Perkins, founder, JustMums Recruitment

Introduction

Hello and thank you for picking up this book. Whether you are a working mum yourself or someone who is close to one, we hope you will love the stories in this book as much as we do.

Working Mums is a collection of empowering stories from Australian mothers. It's about managing the resources we have while juggling work and families. Some of the contributors are public figures; others are not. It is for mums, dads, partners, carers, grandparents and parents-to-be. It's for anyone who has, or will have, a connection with a working mum.

The stories in this book are from mothers in different situations and at different life stages. And while we acknowledge the hard work and invaluable contribution of *all* mums, the focus of this book is on those women who are mums and who also work for themselves or an employer. This work might be full-time, part-time or freelance. Their inspiring stories are very different, yet in many ways they are universal – not unlike the journey of parenting itself.

Working Mums is a book born and raised by us, Danielle and Louise – two Australian working mums – with the assistance of 25 amazing mums who also contributed their stories.

We are not parenting or career experts; we are mums hoping to help other mums.

A note from Danielle

A few years ago, I created a Melbourne event for parents. The Career Ideas for Mums Expo was the first of its kind in Australia. It focused on family-friendly career ideas for mums, and was attended by more than 500 people.

In the lead-up to the event, I came to realise pretty quickly that although there are career options that are perhaps more flexible and family-friendly than others, bigger issues regarding the struggles of working parents repeatedly surfaced. I felt that I needed to find another way to help parents feel less alone and hopefully inspire them through shared stories.

In the 1960s, women in government positions in Australia had to resign once they got married. Clearly, mothers have always struggled to balance career and children. The stories in this book show that while we are certainly making progress on more equitable rights, pay, careers, opportunities and flexible work situations, we still have a long way to go.

We must continue to try to make changes in a changing world. This book is one way Louise and I would like to do that. Lou, you've been a joy to work with. It's been a labour of love. (Yes, pun intended.)

A note from Louise

Danielle and I met when we sat next to each other, with our babies, at a beachside café in Melbourne's western suburbs. We bonded over shared parenting challenges such as extreme sleep deprivation, and shared interests, including a love for writing.

As our friendship grew, so too did our ideas for a book to help other working mums. We knew so many mums (and their partners) who were also struggling with working, or returning to work, and raising their families. We thought that if we could share some of these stories, we might help others.

It became apparent that we could make a great working team. Our skills really complemented each other, as did our enthusiasm.

And so, this book was born.

We have worked on it in moments stolen between the everyday realities of parenthood, relationships and jobs – but we did it.

Thanks for helping me raise our first book baby, Danielle.

1

GEORGE

Creating Australia's first all-female rideshare service

George McEncroe is a well-known radio host, writer, broadcaster, comedian, teacher, mother of four and founder of Australia's first all-female rideshare service, Shebah. Her accomplishments also include working with international humanitarian laywer Dr Helen Durham and other women in Melbourne to have rape established as a war crime.

I've always been passionate about the care and protection of young people. As far back as I can remember, the sight of a powerless person being ganged up on or hurt by larger, louder, dominant forces has made me physically sick. I've always stood for trying to make things more equitable. For listening to the softest voice in the room.

Shebah is a women-only rideshare app that was launched on International Women's Day in March 2017. It is Australia's first all-female rideshare service, getting women and children where they need to go. It is phase one of two apps I'm designing.

Before starting Shebah, I was contemplating driving for Uber to earn enough money to get a loan from the bank to buy a home for myself and my four kids, after my ex-husband and I had sold ours on divorcing. However, the thought of driving drunk blokes around was too scary for me. I registered twice, and twice I pulled the pin.

I'm not a fearful person. I was the spider catcher in my marriage. I was the vomit remover, the debt collector, and the talker-down of drunks and hostile idiots on public transport. I taught Year 9 religious education last period on a Friday for three years. I was not a chicken. But I was not prepared to be sexually assaulted and, to be frank, that's what I was scared of. Not being robbed. Not being murdered. Not being bashed. I was scared of being raped. My daughter and her friends have been very vocal about sexual harassment from cab and rideshare drivers, so much so that they refer to 'feet on the street' as their safest means of moving around their town. This gets me so angry.

I started to look into how many women were taking up this most flexible of flexible work sources, and realised that I must not be the only woman scared of driving men with a few drinks in them alone and after dark. We all know that women take up casual work like a sponge takes up water, especially if that means they can unapologetically turn off the app and turn it on again as they choose. Yet fewer than 10 per cent of Uber drivers are women.

Mum's Taxi is the second phase of the app, which will collect boys up to age fifteen and older men. It will be a family account and a passenger need not even have a phone to order a car. I'm extremely excited by this development. A person can book transport for children or an ageing parent and actually talk to their loved ones in transit without leaving work.

I'm thrilled about how this idea has been embraced, especially by vulnerable people in our community, for example, people living with disability, illness or fear due to past sexual assault. To bring comfort and meet a need that's been left unmet for so long with such a simple solution, by engaging women in such a male-dominated workforce, feels like a natural fit.

Balancing work and family with solo parenting is always hard. I am the only entrepreneur on a government health care card that I know of. But my sons see their dad, and all of my kids are very resourceful. I have learnt to say no, and I'm also getting better at delegating and prioritising. Sometimes you just have to stop and say, 'How many f**ks can I actually give about this?' I call it zooming in and out. You have to be able to constantly change the focus of your lens and keep your eye on the prize. Kids? Check. Business? Check. Racing to the supermarket to buy toilet cleaner to scrub the skid marks off the toilet? Zero f**ks.

When my children were aged five, four, two and one, I had no support structures. I've never had any support structures. I think that's why I can work my four jobs, start a business and look after not just my own four kids but be on school councils, coach a footy team and a basketball team, and do stand-up comedy – because I have never had anyone to rely on except myself. My mother never let me keep a highchair at her house. Nor a nappy or a portacot. She was utterly unapologetic about it. She'd done her child rearing, thank you very much, and was not about to look after grandchildren. She was still a school principal when my kids were babies and my father is still practising medicine. I did have great neighbours, and we helped each other, but I never had a regular cleaner or babysitter, and my ex-husband was absent a lot. My mother-in-law was the most wonderful support person and was there whenever I needed her, but she lived a long way away and was in her seventies, so I hated to ask unless I was desperate.

She truly knew how to care for a struggling young mum – and boy did I struggle. I had terrible postnatal depression after my first and second babies, and my sister took her life when I was six weeks pregnant with my third baby.

My first job was as a nursing attendant for people with disabilities. I felt very useful when I was helping another person feel comfortable. It sounds like a stretch, but that's what also pleased me about being a teacher, a writer, a comedian and a broadcaster. It's finding the common ground where I can bring comfort to others that I feel most at ease with and like my most useful self. I think it's also the most joyful part of parenting. It's that moment when you stick to your guns on something, and your child sees that perhaps apologising or inviting someone somewhere or thanking someone for something brings an ease that comes with connecting, even if it's initially a little uncomfortable. This feeling of connection is now at the very heart of what I'm aiming to achieve for Shebah's drivers and riders. I want them to feel that ease and comfort, as well as a sense of independence and control, and to make meaningful connections with other women.

There are absolutely no easy choices about managing kids and a career. You can have both if you want both. Just know that everything costs you something, and there's a fair chance that while your partner may be praised for either working or staying home, you will be punished for either working or staying home, and will be exhausted trying to do both. You simply have to learn to suck it up.

The thing to be mindful of is not feeling sorry for yourself, but being kind to yourself, and there's a huge difference. One is petulant and childish, the other is adult and will make you kinder to be around, which is better for everyone, including yourself. Go gently. Hardly anything matters as much as you think it does. Are your kids fed? Will your electricity flow into the fridge tomorrow? Have you got money in the bank for petrol? Yes? Okay, breath out and laugh.

My biggest career highlight has been working with the Australian Committee of Investigation Into War Crimes (ACIIWC) to have rape established as a war crime. I was studying my Masters in Human Bioethics at the time, while also working as a community liaison officer with ACIIWC. We were working to gather evidence to support our amici curiae (friends of the court) brief to the International Criminal Tribunal for the Former Yugoslavia, a permanent international criminal court established during the final months of the war in the Former Yugoslavia and to which the first prosecutor appointed was the Australian lawyer Dr Grant Niemann. My role was to find contacts within Bosnian, Croatian and Serbian communities to interview, then organise transport and translators.

I worked very hard on this with Dr Helen Durham and several other women in Melbourne, and the rape kit we developed, which pushed to establish that rape in this instance was an act of genocide and indeed a war crime, is now being used to help with prosecutions in the Rwandan trials. It was a very traumatic but important time in my life, and confirmed for me that four women working away step-by-step with a phone, a fax machine and a good knowledge of the Geneva Convention, could actually change the world.

And we did. A bit. I want to keep doing it and showing people that they can. I can. We can. Chop chop.

I find it very important to prioritise things for myself, so I have a designated fun friend who loves making me do fun things with her. She's like Julie on the old TV series *The Love Boat*. She *always* has me booked for a day spa or a trip to a gallery *and* she makes me pay upfront so that once a month I have to do something just for me. It's been life-changing.

2

SIMONE

Mad Men to feminist: from advertising to job-share advocate

Simone McLaughlin created Jobs Shared to provide a solution for women to be able to maintain their career trajectory after having children. She now works with companies to create a culture of flexibility for all, ensuring it's not treated as a 'women's issue'. When she isn't working on solutions for gender equality in the workplace, Simone is raising her two boys, training for open-water swims, and doing her best to feed her TV addiction.

I'm always a little bit confused about what to say first when someone says, 'Tell me about yourself.' There's a mini fight inside me about whether I lead with the fact that I'm a mum of two or a business owner, or whether I just say something random like I'm a TV addict and would happily watch grass grow as long as it was on TV.

This is something I think about quite a lot, because in running a start-up business I'm constantly putting myself out there as the face of my business. Who I am, and why I do what I do. Am I a mum first and foremost? Does that best define me? It certainly explains the snot smears commonly seen on my clothes and the dark rings under my tired eyes. But is that who I am? It hasn't been for most of my life, but it certainly consumes my life now. Am I a 'mumpreneur'? Definitely no, mostly because I can't say or spell it. So, in the famous words of Derek Zoolander, 'Who am I?'

After much deliberation, I'm going to start with this: I'm a mother of two young boys and one super lazy, slightly rounder-than-average cat called Rosie, and a business owner of a start-up called Jobs Shared, which is a job-share consultancy. Wife of a very supportive husband, lover of sparkly shoes, consumer of TV shows good and bad, and occasional open-water swimmer. The swimming bit is pretty new, but I've done a couple now and it's a bit addictive so it's worth the mention.

I start with 'I'm a mother' because it's the most important job I have, and I'm really proud that there are two tiny, loud, mischievous little boys who shout out, 'Muuum!' when they need a cuddle, or a sandwich, or some milk, or a toy picked up that is literally right beside them. I love it. I love that when I have a rough day at the office I can still get cuddles and smushy kid kisses at the end of the day, and when it feels like the business is going nowhere there's always some unconditional love that can make things better. Being a mum makes me better at running a business because it enforces the balance. I can't just work, work, work. I have to stop to look after my children, and that forces me to step back and take a breath. And because of this, I make better decisions, probably because those decisions are less impulsive.

The other reason I start with the fact that I'm a mum is because if I wasn't, I'd still be happily working my arse off in 'ad land', blissfully unaware of the gender pay gap and the fact that there are impediments to women's increased participation in senior leadership roles, other than simply not being qualified. I'd have no idea that women account for 92 per cent of primary carers for children with disabilities and 70 per cent of primary carers for parents. Or that mothers spend more than twice as many hours (eight hours and 33 minutes) each week looking after children under fifteen, compared to fathers (three hours and 55 minutes). And I'm not hating on dads here. Far from it. But this is the reality we live in, and it's what has led me to where I am now.

For some reason, I always wanted to work in advertising. Actually, no – strike that – I wanted to be a nun first. That was when I was very young and hadn't quite grasped what being a nun actually meant. No one in my family knows where the idea came from because we weren't religious, but I proudly announced it at the dinner table during a family gathering and I have not lived it down since.

But I left behind the lofty ambition of being a nun and set my sights on the glitzy world of advertising. Advertising was great. I met some amazing, smart, talented people, had a job I enjoyed and was good at, and the pay wasn't bad. But then, wouldn't you know it, I went and got myself knocked up and, well, the advertising industry doesn't really do flexible work.

Ironically, women make over 85 per cent of purchase decisions yet they are drastically under-represented in the creative departments of advertising agencies. In retrospect, I should have seen the writing on the wall when I was asked point-blank in an interview if I was going to have children. Alarm bells should have gone off like Inspector Gadget's spy hat, but I awkwardly laughed it off, thinking it was a bit inappropriate at the time and answered as best I could, knowing full well we were trying to fall pregnant but it was taking a long time, so I wasn't sure if it was going to happen for me. Turns out it did, and I was no longer welcome at that agency once said child arrived. And that is when I experienced my first-ever, real brush with discrimination, and it tasted very bitter.

Why was it so bitter? Perhaps because I'm so used to flying under the radar. I wish I could say that I stood out in a crowd, but I don't. (I had a client who thought they were meeting me for the first time every time we had a meeting, for about a month.) I'm average height, brown hair, brown eyes, I don't wear anything too crazy and I'm kind of quiet around people I don't know. I was never top of the class for anything, never excelled in sport, just average in every sense. And I'm okay with that. My husband, on the other hand, is Irish, so in Queensland he has instant cool factor. Also, his name is Finbar, so if you don't recognise him the second time around, you'll remember his name and be like, 'Oh yeah, Finbar, I remember you. Who's that you've come with?' He has an unfair advantage when it comes to people remembering him. But I digress.

I was living a fairly unremarkable but privileged life, with nothing drawing attention to me in either a good or bad way. But all of a sudden, here I was in a career that I loved, that I was doing well in, being told that I was no longer required because I couldn't work full-time. Ouch! This affects people in different ways, but for me it planted a seed of discontent – a seed that grew every time I heard of a new study about women being disadvantaged or the need for more women on boards and in senior management. We need equality and diversity, so why are we making the path to get there so damn hard? Why do we keep researching it? The answer is always the same. More women means better business, greater diversity, better productivity, more money. We need solutions to help us create this change, and we need to change perceptions around flexible work.

There is a great article by Michelle Redfern about the four phases of feminism, which provides a fairly accurate description of what I went through. The first phase is oblivion. I had no idea there was a gender equality problem. Up until losing my job in advertising it hadn't really been on my radar. I went to school, went to university and found a job in advertising; I put in the hard work and I got the results. But then I got asked a question in an interview about whether I was going to have kids – a question my husband had never been asked. Stage two: awareness.

I got the job, however, so it was okay. Then I fell pregnant and before I'd even taken maternity leave I realised my job was changing – just small changes, like how new projects had stopped coming my way or the fact that I wasn't invited to some meetings. Small, but obvious changes. This led to stage three: outrage. This was exacerbated by the fact that my request to come back part-time for a period, to ease my way back into work with a new baby who was nine months old, was knocked back without even the courtesy of feigned contemplation.

And so here I am, at stage four, somewhere I had never envisaged I'd be: advocacy.

How can I sit back and do nothing when, according to the World Economic Forum's *Global Gender Gap Report 2016*, we are 170 years off gender equity? (Through this report, the World Economic Forum quantifies the magnitude of gender disparities and tracks their progress over time, with a specific focus on the relative gaps between women and men across four key areas: health, education, economy and politics.) I can't in good conscience go on about gender equality or call myself a feminist and not proactively do something about it. Most days I wonder what the hell I'm doing. I wish I could just get a normal, paid job, have a regular income, and pretend none of the gender equality stuff exists. But I can't, and it does. And so I guess I have taken the more challenging path, but I truly believe it will be more rewarding.

Today I'm running my own business, raising two young boys and wishing I was a bit more memorable so that I didn't have to re-introduce myself to people all the time. I can see the role I want to play in gender equality, but it's not about focusing on women. In fact, it's the exact opposite – it's about focusing on everyone else.

We won't help women by focusing on the fact that most mothers want to or have to work flexibly after having children. We will only continue the vicious cycle of welcoming women back into crappy part-time roles well below their pay grade, while they work tirelessly to achieve a week's work in three days, not saying anything because they are grateful to have a job with flexibility. This is not a solution!

We need dads to make their caring responsibilities visible. To formalise with their workplaces the days they do school or childcare pick-ups and drop-offs. It's not uncommon to see dads at drop-offs, but it is uncommon for them to say to their supervisors and colleagues, 'These are the days I need to leave early and these are the days I need to start a bit late.'

We need non-parents to request flexibility so they can have a life outside of work. Why should their request be any less important just because it doesn't revolve around caring? If we don't change our attitudes toward flexibility for all workers, we will continue to see ripples of frustration among team members every time a parent needs to leave early. Through my company, I try to encourage other companies to treat all requests for flexibility as equal, and to deal with them as a team. That way, everyone will band together to help and it will open up opportunities for people to step up.

Where once I was having discussions in advertising around how orange the orange juice in the glass needed to be, or if the car should be white or silver, I'm now having discussions around how to increase the number of women in senior leadership positions and how to encourage more non-parents to request flexible work without feeling as if they will jeopardise their careers. Advertising fitted my life perfectly before I had kids, and I loved it. But as they say, kids change everything, and for me they've changed it for the better. I know I'm capable of creating the change needed where women don't have to ask themselves if they want kids or a career, because they know they've got a network of women around them who have their back.

And when women support women, we're unstoppable.

Look after yourself! Have a to-do list that you can check off, but don't sacrifice your mental and physical health just so you can say you achieved everything you set out to do today. There is a reason we are told to put our own oxygen masks on first if there's an emergency, so prioritise yourself sometimes. It might seem selfish to do this knowing your to-do list is astronomical, but your health and wellbeing are important to everyone around you, so don't neglect yourself in pursuit of making sure everyone else is okay.

3

OLIVIA

From high-school dropout to Cambridge scholar

Olivia Slater is a Badimia Yamatji and Whadjuk Nyoongar mother, student and wife. Her ancestral homelands are along the banks of the Swan River, in Perth, and further north near Paynes Find, Western Australia. She spent her childhood in Perth and has spent many years living and working in the inner west of Sydney and the western suburbs of Melbourne. Olivia is the first Indigenous Australian woman to undertake a PhD at the University of Cambridge, which she won a scholarship to.

As a sort of introduction, I'm a Badimia Yamatji gnarlu and a Whadjuk Nyoongar yorga. My mob is all from the southern half of Western Australia. I must acknowledge that without my Badimia and Whadjuk ancestors, I would not be here today. My ancestors fought long and hard for me to exist – for there to be a country for me to exist with. My heritage, my family and my culture all work together to make me, me. I'm currently off country, living in Cambridge, England, taking a Masters in social anthropology at the University of Cambridge. I'm a mother, a wife, a mature-aged student, and I'm from one of the most underprivileged populations globally, living as part of what could be considered one of the most privileged. It is commonly referred to as the Cambridge Bubble.

It's been a weird journey.

I grew up in Perth, Western Australia, as the youngest of four kids. My family is huge – massive in comparison to some. I have ten aunties and uncles, just on my mum's side. I have over thirty first cousins and I've lost count of all their bubs. Growing up, I was lucky to have a group of cousins around my age, as my siblings are a lot older than I am. Outside of family, however, I couldn't quite find a place to call my own. I never fitted the mould of girlhood or femininity, not in my too-tall, not-quite-white-enough body, and not in my anxious, bookish ways. When family circumstances in my teenage years took a turn for the traumatic, my high school was woefully underprepared to deal with me, and at fourteen I just stopped going. Mum and I then moved across the country to northern New South Wales, where I continued to try and figure out where I belonged. I attended high school just enough to scrape through with my Year 10 certificate, but I ended up leaving high school – and home – at sixteen.

I spent the decade between the ages of seventeen and 27 working full-time between Perth, Melbourne and Sydney. I was 22 when I was diagnosed with endometriosis. My diagnosis made so much sense – the intensely painful periods coupled with an almost unmanageable loss of blood all pointed to something above and beyond your average dysmenorrhoea. One morning, post-diagnosis, I felt compelled to call Mum to tell her, 'I want to have kids one day. And I don't think that makes me a bad feminist.' She sighed. 'I just don't want you making the same mistakes I did.' I paused. Thankfully, after a lifetime of knowing my mum, I knew not to take it personally. It was actually kind of endearing. She had her first three children young – in hindsight she would probably say too young – and I was an unexpected addition late in the piece. But I was staring down the prospect of never being able to have children, and I was scared. So I decided to have surgery.

One of my workmates suggested I was worried for nothing and that my recovery from the surgery would be swift. My surgery took almost six hours. The doctors found uterine cells scattered across my pelvis, snuggled against my bladder and bowel. Those rogue cells were cauterised and it took a month for me to fully recover.

I settled in Melbourne in late 2007 and got married on 29 February 2008. A few months later I fell pregnant naturally, much to my amazement. I had just started a new job, and while the timing was not ideal, I was excited.

The new role required me to undertake induction training in Canberra, just overnight. I flew up a few weeks later in that weird limbo of knowing I was pregnant but not yet telling anyone other than my husband. While in Canberra, I had a few hours spare and took the opportunity to go to the National Gallery of Australia. I meandered through the various rooms and stumbled upon Ron Mueck's *Pregnant Woman*, a permanent work in the gallery. She loomed over me at 252 centimetres tall, naked and heavily pregnant, hyper-realistic with her *linea nigra*, tired eyes and overwhelming belly. I stared at her for a long while. *This is how I will have to navigate the world*, I thought. My body is gargantuan enough when I'm not pregnant and it would morph into something absolutely terrifying as the pregnancy progressed.

The pregnancy was as smooth as could be imagined – a little pelvic displacement here, a little chronic constipation there, nothing major to worry about. But I didn't ever blossom, I just swelled. Unsurprisingly, I couldn't find maternity clothes to fit and I spent the last trimester bursting out of my seams. I couldn't be contained. Pregnancy was not for me, I decided. I was much more interested in meeting my bub and getting on with childrearing.

My baby boy was born in January 2009, long-limbed, bald-headed and with no vision in his left eye. Unilateral congenital cataracts affect between one and three in 10,000 babies. It's caused by a random occurrence that happens in the womb – a misfiring of too much protein in the eye during gestation. We didn't know it yet, but his lens was completely clouded, his left eye flashing white in photographs. I spent the first weeks of his life struggling with too much milk, torn nipples and a baby who couldn't latch onto my overfull breasts. I developed chronic mastitis in both breasts, which lasted from a few days after discharge from hospital until I gave up breastfeeding when he was six weeks old. My body, which I had fought with for so long, was winning. My baby and I were defeated. In the haze of those first horrific six weeks, I had missed noticing his lack of depth perception. The local maternal and child health nurse had dismissed my concerns about his eyes not working together as something that, developmentally, happens at different times for different children. So at three months old, I took my son to my local doctor and was referred to a paediatric ophthalmologist the next day. My baby was officially diagnosed; he had a procedure to completely remove his left lens a few weeks later, and we got on with healing.

However, I wasn't very good at healing. I couldn't seem to forgive myself for what I saw as my own failings, in gestation and in my son's young life. I thought that maybe having endometriosis was the universe telling me I should never have had kids.

My baby was six months old when I had a nervous breakdown and was hospitalised with severe postnatal anxiety. He and I spent a month in a mums and bubs unit, under lock and key for the first week. I'm still in touch with two of the women I spent time with, our weird share house hospital space connecting us – mothers who were too crazy for the outside world and our beautiful babies. We saw many women come and go. Most people only stayed a few days, but some of us were really broken.

It's been seven and a half years since my hospitalisation. Popular science tells us that our entire cellular system renews itself over seven years. It's not exactly true, but right now, I feel several light years away from the experience of being in a psychiatric hospital.

The amazing job that I had working with Indigenous family history records during my pregnancy couldn't deal with an employee who now required a great deal of flexibility and health support. I struggled to find the clarity and strength to advocate for myself, to push for the flexibility I now know I was well within my rights to request. All I knew was that I couldn't work – not full-time, not for a long time. So I quit. I decided to do something for myself, to take a breath and rethink what I was doing with my life. I started looking at university degrees, which was something I had always wanted to do, but could never prioritise. One night while googling, I found Victoria University's amazing-sounding Indigenous Studies degree, Kyinandoo. I noted down the name of the student support officer and was immediately taken aback.

The student support officer had the same last name as my

maternal grandmother, which for Aboriginal people in Western Australia connects you to Badimia Yamatjis for sure. I rang Mum, gave her the name of the officer, and asked if she knew her. 'She's my cousin, but she lives in Adelaide now. How come?'

'Are you sure she's in Adelaide and not Melbourne?' I asked.

'Well, last I heard she was in Adelaide. What for?'

'She must be in Melbourne now, because she's the student support officer of this course I want to do at uni …' My voice trailed off and Mum was silent.

'Well,' I said. 'Looks like I'm going to uni then.'

My baby boy was now one, and we'd reached a few milestones between us. He had been fitted with a contact lens and I had completed a lengthy outpatient program at my hospital. I began my studies heavily medicated but keen to engage the lonely learning part of my brain. I met my aunty (who I call aunty as a sign of respect and kin connection), and her children, and for the first time in a long time, I understood where I fitted. The students in my program didn't know me, neither did my aunty or her children, and I relished the anonymity. My relationship with my aunty developed slowly, and seeing her was one of the few reasons I turned up to class. I was incredibly weary and only had enough energy to manage my studies, raise my baby, and work on my health. Nevertheless, I thoroughly enjoyed learning and got good marks, something the teachers of my youth could probably see the potential for but did not have the capacity to convince me of. My undergraduate degree helped me rebuild myself.

After a few years, in the third year of study, I was pregnant again. The second time around I was better prepared mentally, emotionally and physically. I was no longer on medication, but I went back to counselling. I wasn't sure if I would have a ridiculous amount of milk again, but I hired a breast pump just in case. I didn't blossom this time either, just more swelling.

My youngest baby boy was born in October 2012. I finally figured out how to deal with having too much milk (again), and my mental health stayed pretty steady. I finished my degree and needed to again make a decision as to where to go from there. I wanted to do a PhD, I knew that much.

I wanted to dive into an ocean of books and come up for breath understanding more about my place in the world.

My eldest boy was in school and my baby boy was sleeping through. I had juggled a few different part-time jobs while studying full-time in an attempt to financially contribute something (anything) to the household. Considering an extra honours year, which would open doors to further postgraduate study, meant my incredibly supportive husband would have to be responsible for financially supporting the now four of us for yet another year of study. However, he agreed that yes, one more year of study and the benefits it would bring would outweigh another year of part-time work.

I stayed at Victoria University and completed a Bachelor of Arts with First Class Honours – a necessity for my eventual goal of a PhD. Who knew I could write? I then tutored at the University of Melbourne, undertook some work as an early-career researcher for an Australian Research Council-funded project, and ended up back at Victoria University working in the Equity and Diversity area.

Throughout these experiences, I had seen enough to know that I wanted to work as an academic, that there was a distinct lack of Indigenous academics to supervise Indigenous students (particularly Honours students), and that my writing and research had merit.

Through following my personal interest in performing arts and my own heritage, I found myself studying at the confluence of Indigenous performance and performance studies. I took a gap year to work after completing my Honours thesis because I still hadn't decided where to study or, more importantly, who to study with. Instead, I took part in the Aurora Indigenous Scholars International Study Tour and travelled to the United States and the United Kingdom. We visited various universities including Stanford, UC Berkeley, Harvard, NYU, Columbia, Oxford and Cambridge. It was more than a whirlwind; it was world expanding. It made me realise that pursuing study overseas could be my chance to blossom.

Stanford looked promising, but could I fit into their theatre and performance program? Columbia and NYU were amazing, but would the culture shock between suburban western Melbourne and New York be too much for me and my family to manage? On reaching Cambridge, I met two academics who were passionate, engaged and encouraging. I applied to a program I had never imagined I would go for – a Master of Philosophy in Social Anthropology. It ticked all the right boxes – further course work, an incredible supervisor and a focus on visual anthropology. A few months later, I was accepted. I then applied for, and won, a scholarship through the Charlie Perkins Trust, which awards scholarships to Indigenous Australians.

I now had funding, and I had a place in a program at the University of Cambridge. We packed up our lives, rented out our house, sold our car and shipped our pets off to my mum. All four of us moved halfway across the globe – just for me.

I'm now one-third of the way through the Master of Philosophy and have just been accepted into the PhD program in Education at Cambridge. Although I am completely run off my feet, I have found where I belong. It's not at the University of Cambridge as such, but it's within the tertiary education system, with my little family along for the ride, while I sit in a library somewhere reading and writing, writing and reading.

Not bad for a high-school dropout.

You don't have to have it all, do it all or be it all. You are enough.

4

Mel

From actor to creating play-based workshops for children

> *Mel Butel spent fifteen years as an actor working largely for Queensland and Melbourne theatre companies. As creator of playACT – play-based workshops for early childhood – she passionately educates young people in the areas of resilience, social smarts and optimism, and hopes to help little people become kinder, smarter, stronger big people.*

According to Aristotle, avoiding extremes and finding middle ground is a way of achieving justice, or *diki*. The state of *adikia*, on the other hand, is an injustice that turns the world on its head.

When I became pregnant with my first child, my whole world changed. Hardly an injustice, it was in fact a dream that had nagged and whispered at me throughout my thirties. And yet, with the news, the ground immediately shifted beneath me and the sky began to fall. It was incredulous fear that took hold of me as I tried stick after pregnancy stick. That stubborn pink line truth telling over and over while my head screamed *Oh God oh God oh God* in time to my disbelieving heart. I was in a state of *adikia*, the world was swinging on its axis and me holding on for dear life with swollen feet and a growing belly.

My best friend and I were having a baby. We had only just

revealed the depths of our feelings for one another. Oh, how we had been in heady denial about the chemistry, the complicity, the way we inexplicably cored into one another. Such a slow reveal and then bang! An unplanned, unexpected, extraordinary thing! It was complicated, really complicated, but clearly meant to be. And so we began the journey – tremulous, resolute, shaky-limbed, alive and numb all at once. Scary, brilliant change. I was never one to love the middle ground, anyway.

I had been a working actor taking on fabulous roles for state theatre companies and playing to packed houses. It was all I knew and all I loved to do. There was a lot of mirror-gazing, finessing make-up, changing hair, willing the transformation from the outside in. From the inside out there was the opportunity to lay myself open, bring parts of myself from close dormancy to sharp focus, become another human being, transform. There were opening nights, gorgeous, exciting talented people, nail-biting fear, applause. That work at that stage of my life defined me. And it was addictive. It was the very red apple I was always wanting to bite.

Still, it was full of anxiety. I played hard, my whole self in. For some actors, the tap turned sensibly on and off with a role. My tap, however, slowly leaked into daily life, and the intensity of a role, a certain state of being, mannerisms and a rhythm crept on in. I guess some actors leave their roles behind with the make-up and the dressing-room mirrors. I slept with mine, took them out for breakfast, let them grow large. And I sabotaged myself regularly when faced with opportunity.

I used to wonder why. What was I afraid of? Was it success or failure? When it was all over, I knew the answer was success.

I was afraid I wouldn't cope with the pressure, the personalities, the possibilities. I was never ready for it. I needed safe. The risky safe of theatre. And it did feel risky. Not just the risk of judgement, critics, corpsing (breaking character and laughing onstage) or disappearing lines. Also, the psychological risk of the play. Ask anyone who has had the privilege of tackling Blanche DuBois in *A Streetcar Named Desire*. Risky is an understatement. Safer the sense of company, of family, the shadows, the journey. The opportunity to hone, to fix, to better. I was a perfectionist. I was never satisfied. I detailed, fell down rabbit holes, lost sleep over roles.

In that first year of motherhood, as my best friend (now partner) and I worked our way through our great shock and our great joy in equal measure, I found myself relishing being a mum to this beautiful baby boy, but floundering in every other role. I second-guessed myself all the time. I lost my confidence. I shone around my child but felt dull and valueless when he slept, and kept myself removed from other people. I threw myself into the role and gripped a little too tightly. I ceased to dress in my idiosyncratic style of bright colours and clashing patterns and lovely oddness created by endless op shopping all thrown together in a mad out-the-door dash. I was suddenly thrust into foreign roles as caretaker of the house, of providing meals, paying bills. I was functional instead of chaotic but so, so boring. I didn't recognise myself. I missed performing. I missed the play. I missed the carefree quality of the years before, and although I would have traded nothing for the life of my child, I struggled with myself and my identity like the Bunyip of Berkeley Creek staring into that vast billabong muttering, 'Who am I? Who am I? Who am I?'

Fast-forward eight years and my best friend is my happy ever after and we have three beautiful boys. They are in every way our life's achievement together, and we celebrate that achievement in small daily rituals. There is a comfort in a look, in the sounds of the kettle, the piano dancing notes down the bright hallway, and yes, even in the screams and shouts punctuating the air from three very noisy boys. It's happiness. It's home. And with them, I am the best version of myself.

So how did the bunyip find her reflection again? Slowly. With time and acceptance. With counsel and help, both professionally and from dear friends. And with love, strong unequivocal heart-holding love. It was hard. And it was easy. It was life taking its inevitable course, teaching me to stand upright and appreciate the full force that is my life. It was death staring me coldly in the face during childbirth. It was my baby's first deep-bellied laugh. It was undiagnosed postnatal depression. It was small curled fingers on my cheek. It was sleep deprivation and despair and yelling that came from somewhere deep and primal. It was me being accountable for my choices and my life and discovering those choices had led me to a place where I was more balanced, more valuable, more honest.

It was hard-metalled, soft-bellied resilience. I still hone, and better, and fix things. But those things are school lunches and scraped knees and fighting words. I still lose sleep, but I no longer try to perfect my life.

It's not perfect, I'm not perfect and those three perfect little beings I carried into this world are, of course, not perfect. What was that feeling of perfection I chased aimlessly for so long? Who knew imperfection was so peaceful, so happy, so true?

I have never trod a board again and in all honesty, I don't know that I will. I have friends who manage motherhood and performing beautifully, but that's not me. I was all or nothing in a role, and the time that took – the energy, the focus – is not something I have the desire or ability to juggle with my young family. I still miss it, but I no longer need it, and it no longer defines who I am.

These days I create play-based workshops designed to help children aged between kindergarten and early primary school years develop social smarts and coping strategies, to help them bounce back from difficulties at school or home. I teach them to manage their emotions and their busy brains, and find a quiet space and a happy place within themselves. It's education for the soul and a way of helping all children, including the one in seven primary-school aged children suffering from depression, anxiety and other mental health and wellbeing concerns.

Language is powerful, and words can be a great comfort or a weapon. The way we speak to others and the way we speak to ourselves is so important. We need to nourish ourselves with kindness and positivity, with acceptance and honesty. My work with playACT emphasises an understanding that everybody matters, everyone is individual, and everyone has value.

There is a beautiful Japanese proverb that goes, 'Fall down seven times, stand up eight.' It is how we see ourselves and how we treat others that makes the difference. It is how we stand up after the fall that determines our path. I love this work, the idea, and the practice of it. It feels valuable. And as an adult who recognises anxiety in herself and in her children, it feels like

I have found a healthy pathway that fits my life in a very whole way. My life is primarily defined by my role as my children's mother. And happily so. Happiness, after all, depends on ourselves. Clever old Aristotle again. These days, if I have time to find myself in the mirror I like the reflection. It's the reflection of a journeywoman who is finally embracing the middle ground, keeping balanced on a tightrope. And I'm on the journey, holding little hands as I go.

> I have played a game called 'best – worst – funniest' at dinner time with my children from a very early age. It encourages conversation, memory, apologies, listening, appreciation and laughter. Sometimes we really surprise one other with our answers. It is a very simple recount of the best, worst and funniest moments in a day. I especially love when the funniest moment remembered is so funny that it can only be recounted through fits of giggles and snorted milk.

5

Rhiannon

A reality check, wellbeing, and the value of motherhood

> *Rhiannon Colarossi is an ICF (International Coach Federation) certified life and wellbeing coach who loves inspiring mums to nurture their everyday wellbeing. She founded the Wellbeing Web after ten years as a teacher and school wellbeing leader, where she saw the direct impact a mum's wellbeing has on children's learning and happiness in the classroom. Rhiannon has an eight-year-old son and a five-year-old daughter.*

'Welcome to motherhood,' the nurses said as they handed my new baby boy to me before rushing me off to the intensive care unit. I spent my first few days as a mum there without him. A day prior, with seven weeks still to the due date, I was working in my classroom as a primary schoolteacher when I began to experience excruciating pains. I was rushed to the hospital, where they discovered I had high blood pressure and all the signs of pre-eclampsia. The doctor told me that my baby and I were both at risk, and I would have to be induced straight away. I was *not* ready – I hadn't even packed my hospital bag!

Thankfully, our beautiful son Jonathan was strong right from the beginning. I, however, had a partially collapsed lung caused by a diaphragmatic hernia. It was a crazy time … but little did I know that this was only the beginning of a life-changing couple of years.

Fast-forward two months. It was our second wedding anniversary and I was scheduled to have my diaphragmatic hernia repaired. The days following the operation were a blur. I didn't feel well, but no-one seemed too worried. Then, on day four of recovery, a doctor on his rounds realised I was deteriorating. I don't remember the exact details, but that wonderful man discovered that my left lung had totally collapsed. My chest cavity was full of blood and my heart had shifted 5 centimetres from its usual position.

I was going downhill fast and struggling to breathe. I just couldn't seem to suck enough oxygen in (even with the giant oxygen mask). I was literally gasping for every breath. Breathing had always been something I'd taken for granted, but now it was my number one priority – I was well and truly in survival mode.

Eventually, the doctors decided I must go back into theatre so they could reinflate my lung. Waiting for them to prepare themselves (and me) for the operation felt like an eternity. I had never felt so helpless or scared, and I had also never wanted to live more than I did in that moment. As they wheeled me toward the theatre's double doors, fear consumed me … I wasn't ready to die!

I was 28 years old and I was meant to be starting my life as a mum. This wasn't how it was supposed to be. Waking up some hours later, breathing through a tube, I remember feeling a huge sense of relief – I had made it! I had just been given a second chance, and in that moment I wholeheartedly knew what Confucius meant by 'We all have two lives; the second one begins when we realise that we only have one.'

Lying in the recovery room with a breathing tube that would remain in for some time, I used the opportunity to deeply reflect upon my life.

I asked myself three powerful questions:
What had I actually been doing with my life?
Was I happy with how I was living it?
What was I going to do differently?

Over the next few hours, I had many realisations. I realised that I had been moving through life on autopilot, and that I was just going through the motions – school, university, work, marriage, kids ... However, I did not feel happy or at peace with myself.

The biggest realisation came when I learnt that I had been living my life from a place of fear. I feared being judged and pushing the status quo, stepping into the arena, not being enough, and being a failure.

Most of all, I feared living a happy and successful life on my terms.

I knew if I was going to live my best life, I needed to take the reins of my life. In that moment, I begin appreciating and loving myself. I would no longer seek approval or permission from anyone else. I finally felt empowered to create the life I desired.

I was done with playing it safe and following the status quo.

I decided that I was going to live a present and conscious life, be a fantastic mum, have amazing relationships, and make choices from a love-based mindset.

That particular day in February was the greatest gift. Something inside me had shifted and I'm sure that had it not happened, it's likely that I would have continued to do 'what was socially acceptable' and continued living on autopilot.

Now fully engaged with life, I read as many inspirational and self-development books that I could get my hands on. One of those books was *A Return to Love* by Marianne Williamson. The following quote of Marianne's truly resonated with me:

Our deepest fear is not that we are inadequate. Our deepest fear is that we are powerful beyond measure. It is our light, not our darkness that most frightens us. We ask ourselves, 'Who am I to be brilliant, gorgeous, talented and fabulous?' Actually, who are you not to be? ... Your playing small does not serve the world. We are all meant to shine ... And as we let our own light shine, we unconsciously give other people permission to do the same. As we are liberated from our own fear, our presence automatically liberates others.

I loved being a teacher. Empowering and educating the younger generation was so fulfilling. After a year being at home, I approached my boss about going part-time. He was really supportive and said yes. I would go to work two days a week and be with my son the other five days of the week. Perfect plan ... or so I thought.

Jonathan started childcare at fourteen months old, and within weeks he had his first ear infection. After the sixth ear infection, the doctor advised us that he needed grommets. So at eighteen months of age, Jonathan had the operation.

It was a very challenging time. In fact, it was the start of one of the most challenging times of our lives – one that would see us endure a total of six years of severe sleep deprivation (Jonathan wouldn't end up sleeping through until he was three, at which point our daughter was born, who also took three years to sleep through). An average night would entail five to six wake-ups. From the time he was born until he turned three, Jonathan only slept through the night for one month in total. This miracle occurred after sleep school. We loved the month of reasonable night sleeps … and then he got another ear infection! Nine months after I had begun at work again, we realised that things had to change. I wasn't being the teacher or the mum I wanted to be. I didn't want to let the children, parents and teachers down; however, I knew I had to prioritise our family's wellbeing and decided to talk to my husband about the possibility of resigning.

My husband has always been beautiful and supportive, so when I told him that I could no longer continue my part-time role as a teacher, he knew and agreed that resigning was the best decision for our family. Things were just not working! I felt that I was not fulfilling either role well, and for me, being the 'best mum I could be' was the priority. I gave my notice, which was a huge relief for both of us because we hadn't really stopped to breathe since Jonathan had been born.

I was about to become a stay-at-home mum, and although I knew it was the best choice for my family, I wasn't sure how I was going to navigate these new waters.

After resigning, I reflected on my years as a primary school teacher and how they had taught me that a mum's wellbeing directly impacts the child's learning and happiness in the classroom. I knew this, yet I hadn't been nurturing myself. It's one thing to know something and another thing to live in alignment with your truth. My wellbeing was at an all-time low.

I was still recovering from the operation, managing severe sleep deprivation and learning the 'motherhood ropes'. Worst of all, I was not fulfilling the promise I made to myself to live my best life each day.

I had always lived life at full pace and in Wonder Woman style. Slowing down felt strange and uncomfortable. But after the initial adjustment period, I found my groove and the slow time became a precious gift. Deciding to prioritise my wellbeing had granted me permission to simply be and not operate in 'rush rush' mode all the time.

In 2012, shortly after Jonathan turned three and started sleeping through the night, we welcomed our daughter Madeleine into our lives. We moved into our new home when Madeleine was three months old. By that time, she was used to co-sleeping because we wanted to make our time at my parents' place, when we'd be in the same room, as easy as possible. Despite also going to sleep school, Madeleine did not sleep through the night until she was three. The last two years of sleep deprivation while we were still renovating our place, coupled with the financial strain, nearly broke us.

However, each morning I would wake up and decide to prioritise my wellbeing. Some days, simply getting out of bed was a feat. The dishes wouldn't be done until we needed them, however if I had tried to keep the house tidy while running on such little sleep, I would have been yelling a lot. I wanted to maintain my feeling of calm with my family – it was the priority. The dishes could wait, but yelling would cause lasting damage.

I personally don't take pleasure in having a perfect house, in cleaning or doing the washing. I know it comes with living.

What did bring me joy was knowing that our conscious parenting approach was helping guide and empower our little ones to be confident, self-loving, compassionate and engaged learners.

My husband was, and is still, so supportive of me staying home until the children are of school age. However, on occasion, when he didn't have any clean underwear, I was quick to remind him that, 'I didn't stay home to be a maid; I stayed home to be a mum!' He never expected the house to be clean or tidy or for the dinner to be gourmet. We were aligned with our family priorities, thank goodness. At age 31, I felt the happiest and most at peace I had ever felt in my life. By nurturing my wellbeing, I was able to fully engage with life and be the mum that my children deserved.

Every day, I make a commitment to being present with my children. I wholeheartedly believe that that one decision was the main reason I navigated the prolonged sleep deprivation and did not suffer from any form of depression … and my husband and I are still together.

Regardless of whether you are a stay-at-home mum or a part-time or full-time worker, being predominately happy and giving your children quality attention (not your leftovers) is vital. This means choosing connection first, chores second. Fun first, Facebook second. Family experiences first, pleasing extended family second.

When we as mums nurture our family bubble (the relationships in our home), we will truly see a shift in the levels of family happiness … and it all begins with the happiness of mums.

It was with all this in mind that my desire to launch my own business began bubbling away. I wanted to share my wellbeing message with mums and help support them to nurture their wellbeing, not only for themselves but also for their children. However, money was really tight, so in 2011 I began by creating a Facebook page. I started sharing my wellbeing tips and tools to help mums take care of themselves. It felt amazing to be doing what I truly wanted. I was finally living life on my terms, albeit in a small way.

Two years later, in 2013, I officially launched my business, the Wellbeing Web. Hosting my first event was a dream come true and something I would never have dreamed of a few years prior. Shortly after, I became a certified life coach. Studying with the Beautiful You Coaching Academy was one of the best decisions I've ever made. I now felt fully equipped to empower mums to nurture their wellbeing. My business was up and running, albeit slowly.

An Organisation for Economic Cooperation and Development (OECD) report released on 9 March 2017 surprisingly stated that stay-at-home mums 'are our greatest untapped potential and a drain on the economy'. This point reiterates the fact that mothers are still largely undervalued in our society, which may well be the greatest social flaw of the 21st century. I feel we will look back on these times one day in dismay at the way we viewed the role of mothers and their choice to work outside the home or not. Radio broadcaster Neil Mitchell recently hit the nail on the head when he said, 'Stay-at-home mums are helping to hold the fabric of society together.' I wholeheartedly agree. However, I would add that happy mothers (in part-time or full-time work) are also helping to hold that fabric together.

Happy mothers raise emotionally intelligent, resilient, educated children – our future leaders – and that is priceless.

As a society, we need to value mums and the role we play in cultivating the adults of the future. This will begin to occur when we, as mothers, value our precious role. We must openly and actively support other mums in their role as mother and in their work choices. When we as mums support other mums' work choices and wellbeing, we will see a societal shift in how the role of mother is valued. This will be an instrumental turning point in our history.

The way you begin your day tends to be the way it flows. As you wake up each morning, spend a few minutes setting up the tone of your day with a Positive Action Plan, or PAP.

The PAP consists of asking yourself three key questions:
1. How do I want to feel today? (intention)
2. What am I grateful for? (gratitude)
3. What are my top three priorities? (priorities)

The daily PAP helps you to design your day in advance and is the perfect framework for all mums to use as a check-in throughout the day.

6

Jenny

Environmental activism, community and family life

Jenny Weber is an environmental activist and the campaign manager at the Bob Brown Foundation. She lives in Tasmania with her two children Ruby and Finn and her partner Adam Burling, a fellow activist who is Sea Shepherd Australia's Media Manager. They live on a wildlife reserve on 60 acres of conservation-covenanted forest. Jenny has been organising forest protection campaigns in Tasmania for twenty years.

I started life as a mother while I was volunteering at the local environment centre that I helped set up. I had been longing to be a mother for a couple of years and felt blessed to be able to share such a momentous step with my beloved. Adam, my partner, was going to be a great dad. He had already proven to be a loving life partner.

Adam and I had moved to Tasmania from New South Wales to volunteer with the Wilderness Society. When the campaigners at the Wilderness Society chose to focus on the Styx Valley and we were based in the Huon Valley, we planned to set up a new grassroots organisation based on the Byron Environment Centre and North East Forest Alliance.

Adam and I spent a couple of months on a forest blockade in the Weld Valley in southern Tasmania. We had been campaigning for the protection of ancient forests along the Weld River. A new road and bridge over the river was being built to access more forests for logging, and the blockade had been established not long after we opened the environment centre in the Huon Valley. After the police busted the blockade and some activists were arrested, Adam and I spent some time camping at Bruny Island. It was around this time that we conceived our first child, Ruby.

I felt fortunate entering motherhood surrounded by very strong independent women, both country women and activist women – women who had an outlook on life that was deeply based in nature, resilience and a fighting spirit. The environment centre provided a strong community group of people who were older mums from the valley or newcomers to the valley committed to working for forest protection. These qualities really carried me through my pregnancy and into motherhood.

The environment centre in Huonville had been set up by me and a small group of citizens to promote a way of living that included environmental consciousness, to offer alternative products such as paper, cleaning products, plants and all other manner of eco-living items. Central to the establishment of the centre was the desire for these citizens to protect Tasmania's forests – and in particular, the southern forests – from industrial-scale logging. The destructive activities that were directly affecting the community included clear-felling, wood-chipping and post-logging burns – the latter were highly polluting. Then there was the wildlife habitat loss and killing of wildlife, with 1080 poison or shooting regimes.

When Ruby was eleven and our next child, Finn, was five, we closed the doors of the environment centre. After thirteen years of great success as a community-based organising centre, hundreds of in-forest actions and arrests of peacefully protesting citizens, teamed with hate rallies and abuse from local community members and corporations, it was time. We had experienced so much as an all-volunteer-run small business.

I'm sometimes asked about my scariest moments as an activist. There have been many, and they vary greatly. They have included my fellow activists losing hope and – in severe moments of despair – abusing themselves, seeing clear-fell after clear-fell, and the relentless push of the industry machine sweeping forests away to nothing. There was also the fear of bankruptcy due to legal action being undertaken by the corporation Gunns Ltd, who were the primary forestry corporation. Not to mention the ever-present thought of tiger snakes when scouting through threatened forests in summer! Another fear, which some may find surprising, was around the possibility that fellow environmentalists would sell out us grassroots activists and support a corrupt industry – in particular, a company from the jungles of Borneo that I had fought successfully to unsettle in their continued destruction of the planet.

I have remained strong by having a loving supportive family, including my partner, children, mother, brothers and extended family. Also, I remember the love and commitment to good that my elders who are lost to this world – including my dad and my grandparents – taught me.

I have a good grounding for strength in my lifelong commitment to compassion, social justice, equality, community and valuing my freedoms, as well as my deep reverence for Earth.

I draw strength from the ever-present truth that nature is more powerful than us, by swimming in the ocean and wild rivers, and walking among giant eucalypts or in rainforests.

My strength is furthermore built by knowing that there are activists around the world who risk their lives daily, and risk torture to do what I do without these same risks. I remain strong by surrounding myself with people who take action for the protection of the Earth, stepping out of their comfort zone and participating in campaigns, advocacy and actions. These people inspire a great level of strength and resilience in me.

I am now working full-time for the Bob Brown Foundation as a paid campaigner. I am thankful to finally be getting paid after sixteen years as a volunteer activist. My supports as a working mum are my own mum and my wonderful partner. We share our parenting and activism with utmost respect for each other, and a deep love of what the other is doing. Adam works as Sea Shepherd Australia's media manager.

Since our first child was born fourteen years ago, our lives have been full-on, with many hours of community volunteering, environmental campaigning, conflict and politics, exploring Tasmania's wild ancient forests and establishing a beautiful off-grid, straw bale home on a wildlife reserve.

The support of neighbours and fellow activists (some with children and some without) has been instrumental. This has included that of Bob and Paul, Lew and Stuart, and Michael and Paul, with the added nourishing support of Maree and John at the Summer Kitchen Organic Bakery. Their support and passion for environmental protection while valuing family and community support has been sustaining.

There were many days in our children's toddler years when our campaign centre doubled as a parenting centre, with a great group of mothers and fathers who were campaigning for forest protection, and we shared the wonder of parenting our children.

One of the best times in these past fourteen years was showing a group of fifty to one hundred people down to the Weld River for an open day, and seeing our children frolicking in the river after trekking through the threatened ancient forests – the very forests we had actively campaigned for the protection of when we first arrived in Tasmania. These forests were scheduled for logging. They are now World-Heritage protected.

Seeing our children enjoy what we had fought so hard to protect was a poignant reminder of the importance of continuing our critical work as activists.

> I often think of women who are activists and mothers who are facing persecution, threats of murder and torture for doing what they do, or live somewhere with immediate climate change impacts, food and water shortages, and I find the strength to keep going.

7

Jade

A corporate refugee

Jade Wisely is an internationally experienced and award-winning communications professional who helps leaders articulate, illustrate and amplify their stories for greater influence and impact. She is an accredited professional photographer, a published writer and a communications coach.

Becoming a mum very nearly killed me.

It took us three years to get pregnant, which was a rude shock after a decade of Catholic education had me convinced that I'd be knocked up the second I skipped a pill. The waiting was the hardest thing I had ever done. Sent me loopy, even before the fertility drugs had had their go.

A baby was the very first thing I had ever wanted that I could not save, study, train or work for, will into being or control. And I was not happy about that fact. If one more well-meaning person told me to 'relax and it will happen', I might have stabbed them in the eye with a fork. In an attempt to coerce my body into complying and conceiving, I begrudgingly attended a lengthy health retreat detox. Full of overworked, overweight, adrenaline-fuelled, type-A corporate burnouts just like me. I tried alternative healing for the first time, because what the hell, I was desperate.

A reiki master told me to swim in the ocean to make a baby. Pffft!

Eventually my husband David and I gave up scheduled sex, waiting and wishing, and decided to try IVF. To prepare for that rollercoaster, we ran away to Broome, Western Australia, for a long overdue holiday. We swam in the ocean and had sex for fun, for the first time in what felt like forever. I came home to face exploratory laparoscopic surgery. On the day of the surgery, I peed on a stick. Just one line. But they did a routine blood test at the hospital and it said I was (only just) pregnant. Barely detectable, but *pregnant!*

This was my first lesson in mother magic.

My pregnancy was not textbook. I was just 30 weeks in during the summer of 2009, the time of the Black Saturday bushfires in Victoria. My hubby was interstate. It was a stinking hot day and I thought I had gastro. I parked myself on the couch under the air-conditioner with an icy pole and rang Mum. Her maternal instinct had her drive the hour to my place to eyeball me. By then, I was peeing red. So off we went to hospital.

I had the doctors baffled. Turns out my appendix had burst, my system had turned septic, and my kidneys and other organs were shutting down. Not pretty. I had emergency surgery to remove my appendix and a damaged 20-centimetre section of my bowel. Then they sealed me up, sedated me and pumped me with steroids to give bub's too-young lungs a chance. Days later, I went into labour and so it was back to surgery. They did a super-fast caesarean then a lengthy clean-up of my messy insides, including flushing my system with 12 litres of other people's blood (thanks donors).

After all the waiting to become a mum, I missed the big moment of childbirth. I was out cold. I was then in intensive care for two days while David protectively stood by our newborn son's humidicrib. I need not have bothered to read *Belly Dance for Birth* after all. We never even made it to a pre-natal class. He was out at just 31 weeks.

Turns out I am not a great patient. Morphine gives me elaborate hallucinations, to the amusement of everyone around me. I hated being hooked up to so many 'things' – drug drips, colostomy bag, catheter, wound drain, breathing tube down my throat, oxygen mask, IV feeding tube sewn along my collar bone, monitors with alarms, and nurses hand-expressing my colostrum into a teaspoon every two hours around the clock. I begged the doctor to disconnect something, anything, as a sign of progress. To which he replied that I 'should be dead, so shut up and heal'. My next big lesson of motherhood was that I am not in control. I had no choice but to surrender, accept help and allow my body to do what it needed.

By this point, I had lost all faith in my body and hated it for failing me and my son. We were in hospital for five weeks. And when we finally brought our baby home, I packed all the trauma and drama of his arrival into a box and filed it in the vault at the back of my mind. Then I got busy with learning how to be a mum.

My miracle boy, Declan, weighed just 2 kilograms, fitted into my hand, and did not even have the strength to suck. But today he's a clever, capable and very tall eight-year-old and nothing stops him.

Two unexpected benefits of our rough start were that Dave was a hands-on dad from the very start. He stepped up, because I could not, and that meant he was confident and capable. The other was that I never felt like we were raising our son alone. We knew him better than anyone, but we had a team of medical professionals, super enthusiastic first-time grandparents, and a fantastic local mums' group who all loved him too. I was so grateful for their wisdom and diverse perspectives because, goodness knows, this was a bigger job than we could handle alone.

Soon after Declan turned one, I returned to my role as a senior manager at a big bank. It hurt to hand over my precious boy to childcare staff, but they were wonderful and he was happy. I relished toilet trips alone, staying clean all day, uninterrupted adult conversation and feeling as if I was good at something again. But my job did not light me up the way it once had.

Pre-parenthood, I was the consummate career woman. Achievement-addicted. I had two decades of experience, awards and accolades, and a position of influence. I worked hard, happily putting in extra hours so that the job was done really well. I wondered if my newfound lack of career mojo was because I was working part-time. So Dave cut back his work and I tried full-time again. But I still felt utterly unfulfilled – so I changed employers.

Then, in the days between being offered my new role and actually signing the contract, I found out I was pregnant again. Dave and I had assumed it would take time to make a sibling for Declan, but we had been successful within months. So I was mere weeks into the pregnancy and having to tell my new boss, with considerable trepidation. To her credit she was supportive, and so I stepped happily into my dream job working for local government. I worked my butt off to establish a team and get the place humming so that I could step away knowing it was a well-oiled machine. And it worked.

In this process, though, I had neglected to prioritise me. I went into my second birth heavier, unfit and anxious. Again, I surrendered. Another caesarean, but this time planned, and I was conscious. Hearing baby Ben take his first breath and cry out is something I will never forget. We were discharged from hospital days later. We spent those first weeks getting to know each other. And I realised that this was how it was supposed to be.

Ben is joy personified. Such good fun. When his first birthday loomed and my return to work was nigh, I was in no rush. I was having fun, which somewhat surprised me. Our plan had always been for me to return to work and for Dave to take some time off. I was the household breadwinner. But when it came down to it, I did not want to give up my time with the boys, and Dave did not want to be a stay-at-home dad yet. We compromised. I returned to work three days a week and Dave worked four days. And the boys went to childcare for two.

It was all good in theory. But I was bringing work home every night – doing a full-time job but being paid just 60 per cent. I spoke to my boss and arranged to do a fourth day from home. It worked okay, yet they still wanted more of me. Full-time. I resisted. And the pressure loomed large.

I looked for role models, corporate leaders who were also present parents, but there were very few examples. I sought advice and was told to hire a nanny and outsource the home duties. I hate cleaning the house, so this was a no-brainer. But I hated the thought of someone else running our home and witnessing the kids' milestones while all I did was play catch-up as I tucked them in at night. Another well-meaning leader told me to have a work uniform, like Barack Obama, and wear the same thing every day to conserve decision-making power for work tasks. Every fibre of my being resisted this. I relish novelty, and it was becoming abundantly clear that I needed to find another way. My employer offered a part-time role – with a step down the ladder and a 25 per cent pay cut – as the price for the flexibility I sought. And my own mother thought this was a good solution. But I resented the implication that my skills and experience were worth less just because I had fewer available hours. That's insulting and just wrong!

After almost two years of the juggle, I was spent. Leading a team of twelve, a family of four, and neglecting my marriage and my health was a recipe for hell. My dad was battling prostate cancer and I barely had time or energy to help. I was miserable, and yet feeling guilty for being unsatisfied. I had everything I had ever wanted – and no time or energy to enjoy any of it. I was not happy, and it was affecting everything.

I decided to prioritise my time based primarily on what made me happiest. My job did not, so I quit and began a mission to create an amazing life, not just a living.

My boss was shocked. Possibly even jealous. At the same point in her life, she'd chosen to lean in at work and now she was stuck in breadwinner mode and missing out on so much family fun. Some friends cheered me on with curiosity. Others took it personally that I had 'given up' and they no longer had me as a friend who 'understood the battle'. Oh, I understood. I just chose to no longer play that game.

I was a corporate refugee with no plan. And it was exciting and terrifying in equal measure.

Thanks to our delayed start to parenthood we had some savings, and I used them to study photography. This had been an interest of mine since the high-school darkroom. I wanted to hone my craft, find my voice, and become a freelance photographer.

Within two years, I had a six-figure photography business and more clients than I could manage well. I could feel the overwhelm creeping in, neglecting myself and sacrificing sleep and home-cooked meals so that I could spend time editing. Again, unsustainable. But I was flexible. I was in control of my diary (even if I was still learning to manage it well). And the family was much happier.

The flipside of flexible is that every fever, classroom event, sports lesson and unusual happening is yours to deal with. I love being able to help young school kids with reading in the classroom, but I do feel the pressure of trying to run a profitable business and be able to drop what I am doing at a moment's notice. Dave and I both make the assumption that this is easier for me because I am my own boss, but that comes at a cost.

One of the biggest things I have learnt as a working mum is that the greatest weapon of any woman – in business, parenting and life – is self-love. Have an affair with yourself. Make time. Get to know and love the new you. Make space to reflect. I know it can be hard. I usually have too many tabs open in my brain at any time. But you really must slow down to take in the lessons, so you can grow. And when you know better, you do better.

It's much less about the work you choose to do, and all about the person you're becoming in the doing.

I dance – enthusiastically and often. Impromptu kitchen discos and car trip concerts have saved my sanity many times. I dance solo or with the kids. I move, mindfully thanking my body for what it can do. I drown out annoyances by cranking up the tunes. I dance, not caring how it looks (the worse, the better) and focus on how fun it feels. Moving to music is mood medicine for me.

8

Alisa

Sport, business and life

A former world champion aerial skier, Alisa Camplin made sporting history in 2002 as the first ever Australian woman to win gold at the Winter Olympics. After eighteen years as a global corporate executive, Alisa now juggles a mix of sport, business, consulting, charity and governance roles. No stranger to physical and emotional trials, Alisa runs resilience and high-performance programs to assist others to achieve their full potential.

> *For a long time, it had seemed to me that life was about to begin – real life. But there was always some obstacle in the way, something to get through first, some unfinished business, time still to be served, a debt to be paid. Then life would begin. At last it dawned on me that these obstacles were my life.*
>
> – Alfred D. Souza

This quote talks to my heart. It reminds me every day to enjoy the journey and to accept that my busy, chaotic, challenging, joyous juggle is in fact my life! Reading this quote regularly helps me remember to notice and relish the good things, because being a working mum is hard work.

Before I fell pregnant for the first time, I was working

as an executive in a large global corporation and part of a high-performing talent group. I was on an accelerated career trajectory, leading large strategic transformations, closing big international deals and overachieving on the delivery of demanding targets. I filled my days, nights and weekends with my interests – most of them work, and others the convergence of work and passion.

Before that, I was an Olympian. I won gold in Salt Lake City in 2002 (on fractured ankles). In 2006 in Turin, I enjoyed the privilege of being Australia's opening ceremony flag-bearer and then took home bronze (after two back-to-back knee reconstructions). I was the first Australian skier to be a world champion and win medals at consecutive Olympic Games. Along the way, I had some pretty spectacular accidents and injuries, but that's a whole different story. I mention them here, though, because despite the years of hard work, planning and high-performance training that helped me get to the top in one area of my life, I was certainly not prepared for the challenges of being a parent.

I had always worked exceptionally hard to achieve the highest results, and I knew no other life. I loved the challenge and was grateful for the opportunity to work toward and discover my ultimate potential. But motherhood? I couldn't have imagined the growth and gifts that this would bring to my life.

When I fell pregnant in my late thirties, my sense of identity, and indeed my whole life, was full. I certainly didn't comprehend just how different my life was about to become. But then, when my very supportive employer told me that my position on the 'top talent program' was going to change and it became obvious

I wouldn't be part of the following year's promotions, it suddenly all got very real indeed.

Sure, it was all practical and understandable. The guidance was to not stress out – I was still on the list, just not active due to maternity leave (which I had of course requested). The pause button, so to speak, had been pushed. I understood, but there was still that immediate panic and thoughts of 'Am I still relevant?' and 'Will I get back to being in this position?' It was the first time I felt confronted with the reality of how my life might change because of this little person we were bringing into it.

Little did I know that over the next year, that would be the least of my challenges.

Our son Finnan Maximus was born in March 2011. Tragically, just ten days after he was born, our courageous little boy passed away from congenital heart disease. In Finnan's case, six operations over the first ten days of his life were not enough to save him.

And so it was that amid the reality of coming to terms with the physical and emotional trauma of losing a child, I also felt confused about what to then actually *do*. A big part of my journey had been preparing mentally to take twelve months out to be a mother. But you can't really take maternity leave if you don't have a baby.

My husband and I had made decisions and envisioned certain things. But suddenly, here we were on the other side, but not in the place we were expecting. For the first time in my life, it seemed, I was totally treading water and having to make things up as I went along.

I realised quickly, though, that I did not want to rush back to work or cover my wounds by trying to fall pregnant again. Rather,

I wanted to give myself time to process what had happened. So, I decided I would take those twelve months off, to invest holistically in myself, and to set up Finnan's Gift as a charity in Finnan's honour.

Since then, what Finnan's Gift has achieved through fundraising for the Royal Children's Hospital in Melbourne has been truly amazing. Finnan gave us the gift and privilege of being his parents. But every year since, our brave little boy's gift to other children requiring cardiac care has grown bigger and bigger.

When we did decide that we were ready to try again, it took us a really long time to fall pregnant. We suffered miscarriages and false starts along the way. During that time, I'd also decided to develop my own business running resilience and high-performance training and development programs across the corporate sector. And so, my instinct to plan and my inner monologue of 'Where's my career going, what am I doing, how much do I invest in myself and into my own business?' kicked back in. After all, it's easy to tell yourself to live for today and worry about pregnancy if it happens. But when you're making sizeable choices around mortgages, business investment, employee development and your own training and education, it's hard. You question how much of that you should be doing when you're trying to become a parent again.

I like to do scenario-planning, to identify derailment factors and put risk-management plans in place when I'm working toward the achievement of my goals. So this massive thing of trying to become a mother again was like a moving part that I couldn't quite lock down.

I was constantly trying to project manage the timelines and commitments, thinking, 'If I get pregnant on this date, then I can still take on that ...' And of course, as much as I had a spreadsheet, it didn't happen that way. By the time I did eventually get pregnant with our daughter, I was so damn grateful I would have got pregnant at any time!

Unfortunately, it wasn't an easy pregnancy. I was very sick and we also had the fears of another child with heart issues to contend with. But in 2013, our little girl Florence was born, and although she had a small hole in her heart, it has since completely grown over and she is totally healthy.

We were overjoyed to again be given the gift of being parents.

When Florence arrived, I was quite established as a non-executive director working with a number of organisations and I was well underway in running my consultancy business. So going on maternity leave was then a whole different kettle of fish. I had a large number of customers, multiple training and development programs on the go, and a reputation that I'd worked hard to build. I worried that if I didn't keep tending to the foundations of the business I'd lose momentum and everything might dry up. Some other opportunities also arose, making it incredibly difficult to effectively take maternity leave.

One of those opportunities was co-hosting the TV coverage of the 2014 Winter Olympics. I knew it would take military precision to manage, but with the support of my husband I decided to go for it. So there I was, four months into Florence's life, live on national television, working sixteen hours a day while breastfeeding full-time. Thank goodness for make-up artists and fabulous producers, because I certainly didn't look or feel TV-ready!

Florence was feeding seven times a day and I was getting minimal sleep. I was also trying to commit a huge amount of researched information to mind so that I could clearly articulate and recall it live on TV, while not looking sleep-deprived. It was hard, but it was also incredibly invigorating. I had this wonderful chance to share my passion and knowledge of winter sport with all of Australia, and I desperately wanted to do justice to our wonderful winter-sport athletes. It was a true privilege and I would have been sad if I'd let it pass me by.

Because of how things have happened, I've never really known what it's like to take twelve months of time to focus on an infant. For me, it's always been a juggling act.

I learnt the hard way that there is a fine line in terms of how much I could juggle. For example, you can't always plan a conference call for when your child goes down for their lunchtime nap. Despite the merits of a solid routine, sometimes your little bub simply takes longer to settle, and if you're looking at your watch and getting frustrated that everything is not working out, then you end up angry about seeming unprofessional and upset because you feel like a bad mother – all at the same time. And that's when I realised I could only wear one hat at a time and that I had to be fully present in whatever role I was playing, in order to both enjoy it *and* do it well.

In saying that, I definitely knew that by working and pursuing my passions, I was a better mum.

Working gave me breaks, exercised my mind and helped me feel connected both to other parts of me and the rest of the world. If I could regularly step out, then back in, I was also a more tolerant, energised and appreciative mother.

It was a great lesson and I'm kind of lucky I got it early. Now when I'm working, I'm 100 per cent working and I'm guilt-free, and when I'm 'mumming' (which of course is still work) my phone is down, my computer is off and I'm fully engaged. I maximise and cherish my mum time!

Of course, it's not always easy. I often feel like a headless chook running home to express milk and jump in the shower before going to a board meeting, making sure not to put on my good shirt yet because I've got to feed my little one before handing over to the babysitter, and because I stopped to throw on the washing as I rushed out the door I forgot to grab my good shirt, so I had to run back inside to get it, all while having a list of approximately sixteen other things going on in my head.

So yes, it's semi-organised chaos sometimes. But when I step back and ask myself if it's worth it, I can honestly answer that overall, it is. Challenging? Yes. But what era of life isn't?

Another example of how I could never have imagined how different a working life with children would be, was when my car became a pseudo office.

The only childcare centre where I could get a part-time spot for my son had a January intake (yes, we were lucky enough to have a third child). Felix was only six months old, and I didn't really want to put him into childcare yet, but I effectively had no choice if I was going to hang onto my employees and keep my business going.

So I would take Felix into the centre for an hour at the beginning of the day, and in that hour I'd sit outside in the car and do two 30-minute conference calls. I did that for a month before I also let him have his sleep there. He also used to have a morning breastfeed after the sleep, so I would drop him inside, go sit in the car and do two calls and an hour's worth of emailing and writing documents. Then, I'd run in and breastfeed him and then take him home. I worked like this for three or four months, using my car as my office, because driving anywhere would have cost me fifteen minutes each way – and every fifteen-minute block was invaluable to my productivity and output. This level of efficiency would not have been fathomable before children!

Another thing I would not have been able to fathom before children was the true meaning of sleep deprivation.

I remember once being so tired that I just dropped the bottle of cooking oil I was holding. There I was, in the middle of the kitchen, with a litre of oil and broken glass all over the floor and two screaming children waiting for their dinner.

Those moments are so typical of parenthood. They're small, but when they happen day in, day out as you're trying to learn how to navigate this new life on the run, under pressure, and while sleep-deprived, they can be the straw that breaks the camel's back. Your resilience is being tested daily in a culmination of tiny events. It's no wonder it sometimes seems so hard.

And that is why I am so grateful for the sports psychology training I did as an athlete. While I originally learnt the tools and techniques with the objective of winning Olympic gold, their main gift was setting me up with skills for life. Skills around resilience and having a growth mindset, increasing self-awareness and better controlling my thoughts and emotions, improving my ability to focus and manage distractions, learning how to compartmentalise and keep things in perspective, valuing and utilising rest and recovery, and particularly elevating the quality of my self-talk – skills that I now also teach to others through my business. I can't imagine capabilities that are more relevant to the everyday challenges of parenting!

Back to the sleep deprivation that caused me to drop the oil. At that time, with my youngest still breastfeeding multiple times overnight, I was surviving on somewhere between three-and-a-half to five-and-a-half hours of sleep per night – and that was over three broken chunks. Now, I'm not someone who can survive on that level of sleep, but I had to, because that was the reality of what I was dealing with.

Sports psychology became exceptionally important, because I had to be extremely realistic about my situation and very deliberate around my mindset and actions. It can be way too easy to let the emotions rise up, to bundle problems together, to blame or let things become bigger than they really are in any single point in time. Believe me, with oil and glass all over the floor, it would have been really easy to cry for every hardship of the week. But when you are under pressure, taking a deep breath and simply asking yourself 'What is one thing I can do right now to positively move forward?' gives you back control! It elevates your optimism, helps you stay in the moment and channels your focus toward something better.

So I reminded myself that these are the things that happen when you're exhausted, and that I should not beat myself up. Instead, I swept up the glass, cleaned up the oil, and went to bed earlier that night. I chose to let it go.

I don't mean to make it sound simple, because I've had years of practising it. But I know that it works. I know that negative self-talk is self-sabotage so I refuse to do it. It's important for me to try – as hard as it might be – to be a problem-solver instead of a victim when things are at their worst. Instead of 'How did I get here, why is this happening?', I ask, 'How can I move forward?' Sometimes life is just not fair, but with the acceptance of reality you can start looking for the solutions you need.

A key part of my journey has been the realisation that there's just as much growth in phases of consolidation.

Before parenthood, I'd always been on an accelerated career trajectory, whether it was business or sport. I knew no other life. But parenting doesn't present you with the same measurable achievement opportunities. In fact, sometimes it's relentlessly the same, and you feel like you've regressed more than you've grown.

It took me a while to appreciate that sometimes growth is not in advancement, but in breadth and depth – in slowing down, deepening experiences, discovering the richness in patience and trust. It's an important skill to be comfortable with the discomfort, and I teach this to others. You might feel as if you're in pause mode or going nowhere, but consolidation allows you to strengthen your foundations in preparation for your next phase of growth. It helps you to appreciate and experience other key dimensions of life. Now I value and consciously embrace these consolidation phases in life, too.

There are so many ups and downs as a working parent, with plenty of good, bad, great and horrible moments filing every day. I've had to change the way I appraise success and how I conceive my level of contentment in this era of life. In my sporting and corporate roles I had concrete results, such as winning a medal, signing a deal or being exactly at a certain point on a roadmap to a target. With parenting, it's more about noticing the good, banking the small progressions, and tuning into the joyous elements while moving through the frustrations with an understanding that challenge and difficulty are part of it. It's all learning and opportunity for self-reflection and continued growth, knowing that tomorrow will bring another day full of opportunity.

I seek time-averaged contentment now, and ask myself, 'Am I further forward today than I was last week or a month ago? Did I take happiness from the good bits and feel satisfied with how I managed the hard bits? Am I appreciating my efforts and being kind to myself along the way?' This is especially the case in this phase of life, while I have two very young children. I recognise that my current time-average contentment is in a difficult window. So I'm trying to practise patience with myself and my family, and move forward with less anguish and less judgement. I'm also keeping things as simple as possible and only focusing on a small number of priorities.

Overall, my level of contentment is higher because I'm consciously living what I think is my version of success for this window of life right now. A future window will allow a different mix of priorities and a different definition of success and contentment.

As a working mum, I think it's particularly important to sit down and define what your version of success is for the present moment. Try to separate the wants from the needs, be realistic and then make sure you align your priorities, energy and decision-making accordingly. It's much easier to thrive as a person, as a professional and as a mum, if you have clarity. It's also easier to ask for help. In saying that, you do need to think about the whole you and consider your holistic success. Don't be afraid to put yourself first, as your total wellbeing is your foundation for everything else.

I am by no means even close to perfect. There are just as many times I don't get it right, when I am running out the door thinking I've bitten off more than I can chew, or I'm disappointed in my response to a three-year-old pushing boundaries as I rush to get the kids dropped off so that I can get to work. But then, I just have to remind myself that I'm doing the best that I can, for *now*.

And in the end, that's all any of us can really do.

> I know from sports psychology that the last thing you say to someone directly correlates with how their brain will think. When you're coaching an athlete for example, you say, 'Do this' as opposed to 'Don't do that'. You focus on the positive action you want to see.
>
> So I am really careful about the language I use with the kids. If my daughter is up high on a climbing frame, I won't say 'Be careful!', which invites doubt or fear. I'll say, 'Strong hands and strong feet!', which shows confidence and helps develop positive, action-orientated self-talk.
>
> Of course, half the time I miss the opportunity to say and do the correct thing, but it's all a work in progress and the opportunity to keep practising and improving. And that in itself is the wonderfully unique journey of learning to be a parent!

9

Kristy

The Imperfect Mum community

Kristy Vallely is an Australian blogger and business operator who created the hugely successful online community The Imperfect Mum. Kristy created her website and Facebook page after seeing the need for a safe, judgement-free space where mums could talk, engage and relate to each other on the imperfect nature of motherhood.

Motherhood is full of love, sacrifices, good times, bad times, interruptions, never-ending demands and experiences that can leave us drained and overwhelmed. Not to mention the fact that we can sometimes lose ourselves because we are forever putting other people's needs before our own.

When I first became a mother, it was such a shock. I had no idea that I would find it so overwhelming. I remember sitting on my lounge room floor one day, holding my daughter. She was absolutely perfect. Unfortunately, all I could feel was a deep, dark feeling of anxiousness.

I was completely and utterly overwhelmed. I could hear this voice in my head telling me how hopeless I was. This baby deserved so much more. It was like the walls were caving in. It was a very scary time, and a moment I will never forget.

My journey didn't start out like most. We lost our first beautiful baby, Titan, too soon. He was born, and half an hour later, died. Then, with both subsequent pregnancies being high-risk, I spent a lot of time in hospital. The effects of our deep loss and the stress of the high-risk pregnancies changed me as a person, and I believe these were pivotal points in my life.

I started to look beyond myself, beyond my journey as a mother. I would look into the eyes of others and I would feel their pain, their sense of isolation. Most often, I thought about how as a young mother I had such a strong network of family and friends surrounding me. I wondered about the other mothers who did not. What would this isolation mean for them? What would it mean for their children? I wanted to create a place they could go to. A place they could feel safe. A place they trusted.

As a society, we are bombarded with unrealistic images of what motherhood should be, and I think many women strive for this unattainable ideal. I wanted to break down that image. It has a lot to answer for. I believe it can be a trigger for postnatal depression and even cases of child abuse. Our old-style village no longer exists. I wanted to create a space where people could feel safe to ask all sorts of questions, judgement-free. We have all been in situations we are not proud of, or may not want to share with anyone for fear of being judged.

And so, in June 2011, The Imperfect Mum was born, an online sisterhood of women who come together to support each other. It's a safe place we can go to relate to each other on the imperfection of motherhood. Of course, creating such a space meant I had to create a culture, and I knew that would take a whole lot of time.

I gave myself twelve months. I knew it would be hard, but

I never anticipated just how hard. I knew this space was needed but I hadn't realised just how much. So when the gates to the site finally opened, a surge of women burst through.

As they say, 'You cannot know someone or judge someone until you have walked a mile in their shoes'. Ours is a judgement-free place where all women are accepted and encouraged to be the best they can possibly be. The behaviour within the 'sisterhood' can contribute positively to creating a beautiful and harmonious community in which women can be inspired.

Creating this sisterhood and becoming a mum has changed my life in so many ways. Here are just some of the lessons I've learnt along the way.

There's no such thing as perfect

Whether you're a working mum or a stay-at-home mum, there is no such thing as a perfect mum.

Perfection does not exist, yet we're all striving for it. We're all placing so much pressure on 'should'.

We expect that we *should* always enjoy motherhood. We *should* always want to give to our kids even when there's nothing left to give. We *should* be present and ready to engage, play and be there for our kids 100 per cent of the time. We *should* always attend all of their school plays or sports carnivals. We *should* always be patient. We *should* never yell or lose our cool.

Where did this *should* come from? And where did this expectation to be a perfect mum come from?

By wanting to appear 'perfect' to our kids, we are sending them a false impression of what we want *them* to be. Then, they will grow up, trying (and failing) to appear to have it all together and be 'perfect like Mum'.

I think the best we can do is to be honest with our kids. If we yell, fail, lose patience, stress out or fall in a crumbling mess (the list goes on!) it's what we do *afterwards* that has the biggest impact.

My kids *know* I'm not perfect (phew – pressure's off!) but they can see that when I fail, I get back up, apologise, explain calmly (as best I can) why I did what I did, thank them for understanding and get back on track. Which is the exact same thing I'd like my kids to do when they fail. I want them to know that they are not invincible, nor being judged, nor any less loved for 'failing'.

They are imperfect – just like everyone else on this planet. By losing the need to be perfect, we're teaching our kids such a valuable lesson.

Don't compare your journey

Whether we're working mums, stay-at-home mums or any other type of mum, we're all the same.

Do you find your eyes watching other mothers and hear a little voice in your head saying, 'She is so, so much better at this whole motherhood thing than me'?

I do. All. The. Time.

I know we shouldn't compare. But we do, right? (As sad and embarrassing as it is to admit.) But why, I wonder? Why do we compare and judge ourselves so much? I mean, I'm a confident, generally self-assured person, so where does this all come from?

These expectations we put on ourselves are so ridiculous.

You see, in life, we're often comparing our lives to someone else's, especially when it comes to social media. You'll quite often see happy pictures of your friends playing with their kids, or the happy selfie with their husband, or the nutritious meal they've cooked for their family. Or their perfect, clean house. The list goes on. You start to develop this picture – a picture of what you perceive to be their life. When in fact it's their highlights reel.

We're not seeing the sink overflowing with dishes. We're not seeing the fights they have with their husband. We're not seeing the mounting laundry. We're not seeing the dirty and sticky floors. We're not seeing their sad moments. We're not seeing their stressed faces when they open their electricity bill. We're not seeing them losing it and yelling at their kids.

We're not seeing the whole picture.

We can all (including me) easily get stuck in the rut of comparing our lives to someone else's highlights reel. This is a scary place to be, not only for you, but also for your kids and your partner, as you start to perhaps put undue pressure on all of those relationships. We're never happy. And that is immensely sad.

I've learnt that it's so, so important to be realistic with our expectations of life. After all, real life isn't a highlights reel. It's all the bits in between.

My biggest tip would be routine and organisation. I know, it's boring! It's something I struggle with because I prefer to go with the flow; but unfortunately, going with the flow isn't conducive to running a household with little people.

I keep both a Google calendar and a hardcopy diary. I put our general schedule and appointments in the Google calendar and insert reminders that can be emailed. You can also set notifications. I use my hardcopy diary for all my day-to-day jobs. You don't need to have both, but for me it works.

10

Missy

Motherhood, making music, and a changing world

Missy Higgins is an Australian singer-songwriter, musician, actress and activist. She has released numerous number-one albums and won several Australian Recording Industry Association (ARIA) music awards. She also pursues interests in animal rights, the fair treatment of asylum seekers and the environment.

I started playing music and singing live earlier than most – I was about fourteen. My older brother was a jazz musician and I used to sneak into the clubs to sing with his band on the weekend.

A few years later, I started slowly writing my own songs, then when I was seventeen, my sister entered one of those songs, *All For Believing*, into a radio competition called triple j Unearthed. I'd never heard of it at the time (I guess I was a pretty sheltered youth!) but it was a big deal when I won – it led to me signing a record deal on my eighteenth birthday.

I toured really hard, for many years. I even moved to the United States for a year or two, promising myself that I wouldn't come home until I'd 'made it' over there. In the early days, I got recurring tonsillitis because I didn't know my limits. I was touring and travelling too much, staying up late and not looking after myself. Eventually, after my second album, I came to a point where I had nothing left. I'd been going too fast for too long. I'd forgotten why I loved music and didn't feel like the music I made was for *me* any more.

So I quit. I told my manager I wanted to go to university (I'd never been before, and I felt it was a rite of passage I'd missed out on) and do something else with my life. Something *real*. Something more meaningful. Something that could actually make a difference. I enrolled in Australian Indigenous Studies.

Needless to say, studying wasn't all it was cracked up to be. I *loved* learning. My rusty, cobwebbed intellect was being used for the first time in years and that felt really great. But there was so much *other* stuff involved that required discipline and patience and real adult stuff like footnoting every. single. sentence. Urgh. God help me if I ever have to write another opinion essay with footnotes all over the bloody thing. I started to realise how lucky I'd been to have a career in music.

I eventually made my way back to songwriting by collaborating with other musicians and songwriters and writing *about* my writer's block. That helped immensely, to face the problem head-on instead of running from it. I'd also developed a new appreciation for all the people who still wanted to listen to me sing after being away for so long. I guess imagining your life without something suddenly makes you realise how important it is to you.

I met my husband up in Broome, Western Australia. Broome has always been a special place to me, and to him too. It's a little country town where the desert meets the sea, and a lot of quirky, artistic people live there. More often than not, they are travellers, seekers who stumbled across Broome and never left. It has a power like that. It drew me in.

Dan is a playwright, a former librarian and a bonsai lover. We fell hopelessly fast for each other. 'Smoking brakes!' we used to say – because although we were getting carried away, we couldn't help it and didn't want to. Six months after meeting each other and after I'd dragged him back to Melbourne (where he is originally from), we were back in Broome for a holiday. He proposed to me casually in his underwear in the kitchen. I giddily said yes, and five months after that I was pregnant.

Right before I became pregnant I'd just finished recording my fourth studio album, so we had plans to tour not only Australia but also Europe and the United States to support the release. I soon realised, however, that now I was pregnant I could really only tour Australia – and even that would be a challenge! It turns out pregnancy hormones were miraculously calming to my brain and I simply loved life (and touring) while pregnant. I even found it easier to play the guitar as my belly forced it to tilt towards me so I could see the strings easier. I didn't even need a strap on my ukulele as it just sat on my belly! By the end of the tour, I was about six weeks away from my due date and getting seriously hormonal. I remember desperately wanting to finish the tour so I could go home and clean under the fridge. I just wanted to nest.

When Sammy arrived, on 5 January after a 57-hour labour (now that's a *whole* other story), he grinned up at me with his purple little face, pooed on my chest, opened our hearts and changed everything.

I was prepared to take a huge break from music once he was born. I imagined not feeling inspired or motivated for many years and just concentrating on parenting – but it wasn't the case at all. Something about being suddenly flooded with raw emotions and new perspectives made me want to write songs.

When I saw the picture on the news of the little three-year-old, Alan Kurdi, washed up on a beach in Turkey after the refugee boat his family had been on capsized, my heart was torn in pieces. I lay on the living room floor crying until I couldn't cry any more. For days I was numb, unable to get the image out of my head. Then eventually I decided I needed to do something with this sadness and anger at our government for treating these people like criminals when all they're trying to do is survive. So I wrote *Oh Canada*, a song about the Kurdi family, told from the perspective of the father, Abdullah, wanting to find a safe place for his family to live. I teamed up with the Asylum Seeker Resource Centre (ASRC) to release this song and donated 100 per cent of the profits to them. Since then I've become an ambassador for the ASRC and I try to raise as much awareness as possible about the plight of refugees.

Another thing that became even more real for me after having a child was the reality of climate change and what that means for Sammy's future. I'd always been conscientious about helping the environment but it meant something new to have made, all of a sudden, a little human who will inherit your mistakes.

I became obsessed with literature about climate change, especially post-apocalyptic fiction about the various dramatic ways the world might end due to environmental collapse. It was bleak, but it helped in some macabre way. Eventually this obsession turned to my songwriting and I decided I wanted to start writing songs about climate change and all the possibilities for our future. I'm a little ashamed to say that a lot of the 'possibilities' I put forward in my songs aren't the most optimistic … but what can I say, I'm a songwriter not a motivational speaker.

Working these days looks very different from what it used to look like for me. I now write in sporadic bursts, and only when I can get someone to mind Sammy for a few hours or when our nanny (who we have one day a week) can take him to the museum. My husband Dan, being a writer, also has very flexible hours so we take it in turns with Sammy, and also have wonderfully generous and helpful parents. Every week is a new set of people taking him for different times on different days. We work it out as we go and work opportunistically. It's not conventional but it works for us.

I know I'm never going to be able to tour as much as I used to, or even write as much as I used to – but I do know that when I *do* write or I *do* tour, I appreciate it more. I appreciate it more because it's *me* time, and that is few and far between these days … and also because I want my kid to be proud of his working mother. I want him to see me happy and thriving and being a strong, independent woman. Then one day when he's older and he meets a woman (or a man), he can remember what his parents showed him – about doing what makes your heart sing, and what makes you feel alive – and he'll feel okay about doing it too.

I've learnt to feel okay about our unconventional lifestyle, with so much travelling, swapping houses, minders and so on, because ultimately all that matters is that your child feels loved and safe, wherever they are and whoever they're with.

11

CHRISTINE

The value of volunteering in creating opportunities

Christine Jolly is an American-born dreamer, juggling motherhood and her passions. She moved to Tasmania in 2007 after finding love on the internet and hasn't felt the itch to leave ten years later. Her current career path is built on skills she learnt after becoming a mother.

The BBC once explored what would happen if a typical British family lived as a typical German family in *Make Me a German*. A husband, wife and two small children all immersed themselves in German living. They lived in an average flat in the city. The husband worked in a coloured pencil factory. The wife became a *hausfrau*, staying home with the two little ones, taking the oldest along to forest kindergarten, catching up with other mums and their toddlers for play dates and cleaning the home for up to four hours every day.

The mother, who enjoyed her career in the United Kingdom, was perplexed. On one hand, Germany was very generous to young families, giving them a monthly stipend of *Kindergeld* (an allowance for families with children) so that a family could comfortably live off one income and the mother could stay home and look after the children. On the other hand, the set-up complicated matters for women who enjoyed their careers and were not interested in putting their career on hold to take two whole years of maternity leave. Even during the primary school years, if a family did not have the support of grandparents nearby, who would be home when the children came home from school at 2.30 pm? Combined with a national stigma of working mums being *bad mums*, it is no wonder only two-thirds of German mothers work.

Born to United States army officers, I grew up in Germany and this complex dilemma of work–life balance plagues me. I am a driven individual, scheming new projects all the time. Yet I am massively drawn to my home life, never venturing very far and always home at 2.30 pm to pick up the kids from school. As a result, my empire bubble has a very small radius. But it's a mighty bubble nonetheless.

While studying for my masters, I met my husband through our blogs. To my shame, I'd never heard of Tasmania, but a year later, I was a newly married Tasmanian living in Hobart. Two years later, I was a mother of a Tasmanian, and then again the following year.

None of my friends were surprised when I told them I'd fallen in love on the internet and was moving to the complete underside of the world. 'Of course you are,' was the standard reply. I suppose I had a reputation as a thrill-seeking storyteller, a globetrotter. I warned my fiancé: 'I'm just letting you know that while I'm happy to uproot and relocate to Tasmania, I will likely get the two-year itch.' Living in a different country every two years had become an unshakeable drive connected to my biological clock. I'd become restless, yearning to travel, experience new cultures and meet new people.

After three years in Tasmania, the itch still hadn't come, and here I was with a small family far removed from my own immediate network of support – parents still living in Germany and extended family and friends in the United States. I was, however, surrounded by a wonderful community of other young families in our local church, all happy to share their lives with one another as surrogate aunties and uncles and sources of parental wisdom and advice.

Most young mums I met were like me: not from Hobart. Many were from interstate, overseas, or even from the north of the island state. They'd moved here for work opportunities or a tree change. They were sold on the idea that Hobart was a great place to raise kids. However, their mum didn't live two doors down, able to pop around and lend a hand with the washing. You couldn't drop your darlings off at your aunty's house while you did a few hours of running errands. Your own best friend was only accessible via the phone or Facebook. Too many of my fellow mums were battling to learn the art of parenting on their own, making it all up as they went along, struggling with the lack of support.

This common struggle came up time and time again. What could one woman do to make a difference to thousands of lives? In 2011, I created a Facebook page: Hobart Mums Network.

I envisioned me and my twenty friends with young children sharing recipes and activity ideas on the page. We'd plan picnics and outings. They'd invite their friends along and our community would grow to a whopping fifty mums. I completely underestimated the scope of the need I had tapped into.

Over the first month, I posted questions they had and the community answered and lent their support. Friendships began to blossom between regular page participants. In thirty days, my vision of fifty mums had become five hundred, all craving connection to a larger community.

Six months later, over a thousand mums who had connected online longed to transition to actual in-person interaction. I planned monthly networking events for the mums featuring a different theme each month: speed friendship dating for mums, a Q&A session with five prominent local mumpreneurs, a health and wellbeing expo, a clothing swap and more. If anyone had an idea – 'Hey, wouldn't it be cool if Hobart had xyz for local families?' – I would be there to say, 'Yes, let's do it!'

One of those ideas was a space in Hobart's shopping district where local families could come, relax and enjoy a cup of tea while their little one played with toys and they could engage in adult conversation with new friends. Not a big play centre, but more of a home away from home. Thus, the Haven was born.

I shared this dream on the Hobart Mums Network Facebook page in April of 2012. Thousands lent their virtual enthusiasm for the concept. Three days after posting, a local business owner, who was herself the mum of two little girls, offered the basement of her retail shop for the Haven. I went to visit the space. It was perfect. Our entrance would be off the main street and accessible for prams. We could have free reign of the space. Make it our own. It was really happening!

In six months, we transformed the space with donations from the local community. A local designer volunteered her time to create a mural for our wall. A local handyman installed a low chalkboard covering the length of one of our walls. Lovely sofas and cushions and toys were all donated by local families. We opened our doors in October with the state's Minister for Women, Cassy O'Connor, cutting the ribbon at our grand opening.

Over the next two years, I said yes to so many other projects. A local group for business mums to network, brainstorm and support each other? Yes! A choir for mums? Yes! Regional book clubs for mums? Yes! A fitness group for mums and their little ones together? Yes! A beautiful cookbook, completely Tasmanian, from its printing to its design, contribution, testing, advertising, photography and project management, all supplied from Tasmanian mums? Yes! An app for local mums to connect to their wider community? Yes!

All of this was as a volunteer.

In 2014, I received a phone call from Child Health Association Tasmania. The board had taken notice of our projects and regular activities and extended an invitation to me and Hobart Mums Network to join their organisation. To be honest, I hesitated. Hobart Mums Network was my third baby. Could I really trust its care into the hands of this organisation? On the other hand, the network was meeting the need of thousands of local families to connect, encourage and inspire one another. How long could one person reasonably continue to drive the network forward? It was more important to me that this level of engagement and support would be available 25 years in the future when my own girls became mothers than for me to continue solely handling the reins of Hobart Mums Network. I released control and joined the organisation on staff as their Southern Regional coordinator.

The transition wasn't seamless. There were bumps along the way as boxes needed to be ticked for insurance purposes and codes of conduct developed for members. However, as we celebrate the centenary of Child Health Association Tasmania in 2017, the organisation and Hobart Mums Network are better for it. Being accountable to a board of management has been the biggest blessing. I know that they have my back, and I can rely on them to point me in the right direction.

I brought skills to the organisation that increased their reach across the state. I maintain the Child Health Association Tasmania website, creating promotional images and videos, managing their social media and publishing weekly 'What's On' emails, connecting members of the community to local events and our regular activities. I also arrange advertising with local businesses, which helps to fund our now two Havens (in Hobart and Launceston), and our annual first aid information sessions for carers of infants and toddlers, among other projects.

Connections built through my new position led to other personal projects. I now lead a series of workshops in local schools for girls, passing on lessons in resilience, confidence and friendship. I also conduct leadership workshops in local high schools.

On top of all of that, I now also own and operate two businesses based on the skills developed since becoming a mother. Jolly Online Solutions is built on the skills I learnt in creating and maintaining websites, e-commerce and online publication. The other is Cradle 2 Kindy Parenting Solutions, which I took over from a Mothercraft nurse in Sydney. My aim is to grow the business to become a worldwide network of parent coaches, delivering up-to-date information on infant and childhood development.

My current career choices were all made while being the mother of small children. I built a local empire of local families, with my two little girls involved every step of the way. My little 'business associates' joined me at meetings at the Town Hall. They played with sticker books while I gave presentations to local service providers. As they began to attend school, my time became more focused on delivering better programs to local families.

But all that stops at 2.30 pm. That's when I turn off my career and I pick up my girls from school. That's when we play on the school playground for an hour after school. That's when we go home for afternoon tea. That's when we read on the sofa. That's when we make dinner. That's when I give them cuddles at night. That's when my husband and I wash the dishes together. That's when we watch the late-night commentators on American politics together. And that's when we scheme together how we're going to make an even bigger impact on our little patch of the island.

It's been ten years. And I can safely say, the itch has been cured. I am perfectly happy where I am.

> My husband and I share one car. We 'book' the car when we need it, in a shared digital calendar. If one of us books the car, the other will either work from home, ride a bike or take public transport.

12

Annie

Blogging and wearing a suit for a bully-free Brownlow

Annie Nolan is an equality activist, social commentator and author of the popular Uncanny Annie blog, on which she writes about parenting, relationships, equality and health. She attracted significant media attention when she chose to wear a suit, as opposed to the traditional evening gown, to the 2016 Australian football Brownlow awards.

I grew up in a small farming town in the Western District of Victoria, Australia. I was always the eccentric, animal-loving kid. I raised money for my mouse's $200 tumour to be removed, walked around with a chicken in a makeshift sling around my neck, nursing its broken leg, and even had a 'rehabilitation centre' for snails that had accidentally been stepped on. My parents described me as 'intense'.

I was also bullied extensively throughout my adolescence. This culminated in an incident that left me with a permanent visual disability. It means I can't drive a car, read a menu, or recognise faces immediately, among other things. I don't often write or talk about it. I'm definitely not ashamed of it, but I feel there are so many fantastic disability activists and writers out there that my own experience is comparatively very little.

I still feel uncomfortable talking about the bullying, despite it being more than a decade ago. Upon reflection, I know I was bullied because I was eccentric and a girl with an opinion who wasn't willing to back down even when people tried to force me to. The day I graduated school was one of the happiest of my life. I didn't care about scores or what the future held. I was just so excited that it was over and I could escape.

Unfortunately, many of the issues I faced back then have continued in my life today in my work as a blogger and social commentator. The only difference is that now it isn't physical or from people I know, but rather from faceless bullies online. I'm often told I'm a terrible mother, that I'm ugly, that my husband is weak for putting up with me – even that my children would be better off if I were dead. That, along with rape, death and assault threats. In absolutely no way is any of it acceptable, but I feel I cope quite well with online bullying because of my experiences growing up.

Sometimes I cry, sometimes I find it hard to sleep, sometimes I have to book in for professional help. None of that makes me weak. It only means I'm human. I recognise that one of my strengths is that I do feel and that I have the resources to continue.

I met my husband Liam in what was then rated the worst nightclub in Australia, according to credible sources (some revolting men's magazines). It was a fast romance and we quickly became a prime example of 'opposites attract'. Our personalities, interests and talents are at polar opposites. However, what we have in common is our ethics. This is the key to why we 'work'.

It was on our first date, as I quickly and embarrassingly explained why I couldn't read the menu and he – without hesitation or comment – picked it up and started reading the non-animal options, that I realised I was sitting with someone special. From that moment, my life got so much better because he was in it. I will always consider the moment I met him as one of the luckiest of my life.

In 2010, when I was 21, we found out I was six weeks pregnant. It was unplanned. It was a Tuesday. The following Friday, my brother passed away in a terrible car crash. He was my best friend and only eighteen when he died. So, being pregnant quickly became the second-biggest news. All my energy went into grieving the loss of my brother. It was only at about sixteen weeks that I fully grasped that I was even going to have a baby. A part of me even thought the pregnancy wouldn't progress, because I couldn't believe that a foetus could withstand being in my body with the emotional pain I was enduring. It was an intense period, and one that I still feel profoundly sad about.

Most people expect that their first pregnancy is a time of joy, but for me, it was a very grey time. I was consumed with grief, and when I finally came to terms with the fact that I was having a baby, I was terrified of the implications for my life and Liam's. But Liam was incredible. He sat beside me for hours trying to spoon soup into my mouth when I couldn't eat, and he'd remember appointments when I couldn't think of anything except my brother. He even stepped up to carry my brother's body out of the church when most others, due to their grief, were unable to. And years on, there are moments that seem like magic, as he instantly wakes as I try to silently cry myself to sleep. He talks about my brother like he is still present, which comforts me greatly, although it also makes it seem so unfair because I know they would have been best friends.

I think being pregnant and having Malachy gave me a reason to get up, shower, get out of the house and look after myself. It helped me at a time when my life could have taken a different turn. I absolutely refuse to ever 'get over' what happened to my brother, and I cannot take any positives out of his death. Nevertheless, a new piece of happiness grew inside me after Malachy's birth, even if it will never replace my brother.

My wonderfully supportive husband, a professional AFL footballer, is an introvert. Quiet, unassuming, modest, humble. I once heard one of his teammates describe him as 'humble on steroids', and I think that is fairly accurate. He doesn't like attention and doesn't do anything for praise or fame. Because he is like that, I often do all the bragging for him. At times, I get carried away with how proud I am of him and embarrass him.

We are so lucky to have football in our lives. Not only has it given us so many friendships and memories, but also my husband is living out his childhood dream in front of me. Although I have rare pangs of jealousy, as I had to put my career on hold to prioritise our children and his career, I love him so deeply that his happiness increases my own. And probably more practically and fairly, he would do the same if it was the other way around. And now that is beginning to happen as my career is taking off. He has had to make sacrifices for my career, and this fairness in our relationship is paramount to us both.

Football can, however, be difficult on my career. For example, despite AFL moving forward with inclusion, such as through the creation of the women's AFL league (AFLW), sexism is still rife.

I will write something in the media or on my blog, for example, and immediately be dismissed because, to many, I'm just a 'dumb blonde WAG' who slept her way to where she is. It's infuriating and an unwanted label I will no doubt have for life. Over time, and after being so vocal about sexism, media outlets even started labelling me 'the Anti-WAG', which I'm not entirely comfortable with either. Although well meaning, I feel the term has morphed to the point that it's negative no matter how it is presented. My friends and I, whose partners happen to play football, shouldn't be identified and valued in relation to who our partners are. We aren't an extension of them – we are working, thinking, feeling people worthy of the respect that all people should be given.

With our next pregnancy, I went into early labour. I called Liam and Mum to come immediately to the hospital and my best friend to watch Malachy. I was examined, and because my cervix had already flattened out and dilated slightly, I could not have a stitch put in to keep it closed. I was given an array of drugs to try to stop the labour (and calm me down), but this resulted in me hallucinating! Liam called to ask which room I was in and I gave him the wrong room number. He ran into the room I told him and witnessed another woman mid-push, giving birth. It was the only funny part of the whole experience, to be honest, because not long after Liam's arrival, my daughters were born – thirteen weeks early.

I clearly remember Liam next to me in the theatre, jittery, sickly, pale and silent. The total opposite to the elation he'd shown at our first child's birth. I kept whispering to him that as soon as the babies were out, he had to take as many photos as he could. He only had an old iPhone on him because we were completely unprepared and, let's face it, photos weren't the main thing on his mind. Nevertheless, I needed those photos because I was terrified that the babies wouldn't make it, and the photos might be all we were left with.

We silently awaited the welcome cries of our twins. We heard nothing. They were so small that their voices couldn't be heard over the machines. I then saw one twin being whisked away across the room in a plastic bag. My heart sank and absolute fear set in. Had she died? Why was she in a plastic bag?

I pushed Liam to take photos. I could see he didn't want to. He was only gone for two minutes before returning. Weeks later, he told me that one of the nurses had told him, 'This is really life and death at the minute' when he went over to see the girls as they were being ventilated.

The birth was terrifying. It's difficult to admit, but I didn't have any rush of endorphins or immediate love for my girls. I only felt adrenaline and fear. We didn't send out an announcement to say they'd been born; we were unable to touch them and only viewed them through their humidicrib. Visitors were limited, and I immediately started expressing milk for the twins while feeling guilty that I wasn't spending enough time with Malachy.

Liam went back to work for several days, and most people didn't even know the babies had been born. He didn't really want to talk and just went in, got the job done and went straight back to the hospital to see the girls. That was his way of coping.

Weeks then months went by, and I was thrilled to see my babies grow and to finally fall in love with them. Every small step felt like a giant premmie baby leap. They got their 'I've reached 1 kilogram' badges on their cribs in the hospital, started suckling, and began to have periods of breathing without assistance. I would often arrive at the hospital and stand outside the door just to watch Liam and the nurses talk and sing to them and tell them how much they were loved. Moments like that got me through. Also, my energetic two-year-old son surprised me with how much he could comprehend and how he could actually sit calmly at times.

After many months, the girls were able to come home. It was the slowest car ride I have ever had. Because it had been hard letting other people look after my children for so long, I felt grateful to change their nappies and be vomited on!

How I feel about parenting and myself has evolved as different phases have come and gone. I do, however, distinctly remember thinking one day, 'This just isn't enough for me.' I was run off my feet with my children but I was profoundly bored. I loved the time with them but I needed intellectual stimulation and adult interaction. Heck, I even needed a laugh. Going back to study or gaining a career outside the home wasn't an option, but my friends and family would suggest, 'Annie, you quirk, you need to put these thoughts and stories out there. Start a blog!'

It seemed so self-indulgent to start a blog, and I really doubted that anyone cared what I had to say. But that was even more reason to do it – to find self-acceptance, to listen to others and to learn. So one day, I just leapt straight into it.

The name Uncanny Annie encapsulated how I felt about myself and the page. 'Uncanny' usually means 'strange' or 'weird', just as I had often felt growing up. However, it can also mean 'astonishing' and 'remarkable', which was what I strived to feel about myself and my work.

I write about parenting sometimes because that is part of my life. But more often than not, I share my opinions on other things, including feminism, politics and equality. Sometimes I just share light-hearted humour or general observations. I've made mistakes along the way, but part of the reason I began Uncanny Annie was to learn, and not to beat myself up. I never delete comments that I've made. I am willing to expose my flaws. I do most of the writing, but I hate 'preaching', so I encourage people to challenge me and feel comfortable giving their opinion. I strive to be inclusive. It's all another way to learn.

And the irony is that, through embracing my differences, I've realised there are so many others just like me. It's *uncanny*.

In 2016, my husband had the opportunity to play in the historic Western Bulldogs' winning grand final. It was an incredible time for my family. Just before the final, he was invited to the Brownlow Medal. For anyone unfamiliar with the Brownlow, it is the awards ceremony for the best and fairest player in the AFL. You have to have had a great season in order to attend, with only five players from each team invited. So it is an honour, and I was proud to be able to stand by my husband, as we have for each other on so many occasions.

However, the Brownlow has also become known as the 'Gownlow', alluding to the situation of the players' partners getting most of the attention, with the emphasis on 'who they are wearing' and therefore, perhaps, the 'trophy' the player 'scored'. Many women enjoy this aspect of it because it helps their fashion careers, but the majority are overwhelmed and forced to be objectified. There is really no opting out. Some argue that the partners shouldn't go if they don't like it, but to me, that's pathetic. It is an awards night we are proud our partners have been invited to. We shouldn't be bullied into staying home. In other words, the bullies should change, not those being bullied.

The invitation stated, 'Strictly black tie and evening gown'. So I played by the rules and went to the Brownlow in black tie, twinning my husband.

The black suit I wore and the 'bully-free Brownlow' campaign challenged people to think about the way the women attending the event were being treated, and the patriarchal system that a lot of football still holds on to. I'm not going to deny I felt empowered when I wore the suit, standing beside my husband in a united gesture of equality.

Predictably, horrendous comments ensued. Plenty about me 'wearing the pants' in the relationship, which was pathetically schoolyard and missed the point that we were both wearing pants. Many comments were transgender slurs, and there were comments about me menstruating and not being able to fit into a dress, how unattractive I was, questions about our sex life, how if I was their 'missus' they would lock me up in a cupboard at home. The best of the internet truly came out to play. I also turned up in the 'worst-dressed' columns in the media. Of course, Liam wasn't in any fashion pages, even though he and I wore matching suits – literally the same suit by the same designer.

But Liam and I were never going to pretend that we thought we could both turn up wearing suits and fly under the radar. Unlike previous years, when I would have worn a dress the same as the backdrop to camouflage myself, this time I wore my outfit to be noticed. And so did shy, media-hating Liam, because he believed in the stance I was taking. We wanted people to stop and think about why I would be wearing a suit, about how we treat women attending the event, and the clear double standards and sexism at play.

I acknowledge that the reason I was able to even do what I did that night was because I don't get worried about these types of comments. But many of the women walking the red carpet are negatively impacted. I have a friend who didn't leave her house for three days after the Brownlow because of the media and comments. And that's why I felt I had to do it.

Don't get me wrong: equality for the partners of footballers is hardly high on the list of humanity's pressing issues. Nevertheless, if there is an opportunity to challenge inequality in any capacity or opportunity, I think it should be done.

I'm glad I did it. I'm even more glad to see attitudes changing because of the many women, players and people who have spoken out as well.

Gaining newfound attention has come with a side of backlash, but mostly it has delivered far more good than bad. It has meant that I can use this modest platform not only to build a career for myself, but also to promote and give voice to others who I believe need it more than I do. This year, I have managed to co-create an LGBTQI football pride game in my hometown to start conversations around issues of sexuality, gender and mental health, particularly in the country, where support is far less available and the struggle is far too difficult for many. Being 'different' in the country can be hard, and I want the country saying of a 'fair go' to live true, and for all people to feel included. In many ways, I have found the power to correct some of the injustices I witnessed growing up.

I am honoured to have the opportunity to do this – to set up the metaphoric 'mic stand' for issues I believe in, then pass the microphone to those who need it most. Not only does it give me a positive outlook for myself and my family, I also feel I'm contributing something meaningful and purposeful. This is rewarding for me on a personal and professional level, but it also helps me feel that as a mother, I am doing my bit to inspire my children to be kind to others and live lives that are meaningful to them, too.

Unfortunately, bullies exist outside of school. They're everywhere, and it sucks. But you can become stronger by learning new and much better ways to cope. Get the right allies. Get counselling if you can. You'll be more comfortable being yourself, and remember that you aren't alone in all of your experiences.

13

MARIA

Building a business as a sole parent with a baby

Maria Smith is the CEO and founder of the successful training and coaching business Bounce Australia, which has expanded into the United States and New Zealand. She is also the co-founder of MyAlura, a company that sells fashionable, functional laptop handbags designed especially for women.

Do you ever feel lost, disconnected or like everything is just too hard? Lack the motivation or desire to change your life, even though secretly you want to, but it all just seems too hard? You get an inkling of what you want to have, feel, do or be, but the idea of moving toward it just seems so far away. It's like the dream is so seductive, but the harsh reality of not having it makes it seem that much more out of reach. If you are like so many of us, you just put your dreams and desires on the backburner. Putting others first so that you can just get by. Feeling you're better off just sticking with the norm and not making too many changes. Plus, everyone around you expects you to just be this way. Why change now?

This was me, this was my path. Years ago, I found myself in a situation where I was lost and directionless and in a relationship that was toxic, scary at times, and empty and painful. I didn't like my job and I had dreams of having my own business helping people, but they were only dreams. I just got comfortable working and getting paid. At least I could pay bills and save a little, even though I felt a deep sense of loss, as if something was missing. I remember thinking, *Well, this is all there is,* and that I couldn't possibly have anything more. I had this nagging voice in my head saying, *You should be grateful for what you have. At least you have a job. At least you have a relationship and you're not alone. Get over yourself, Maria. Be grateful.* This mantra became my way of numbing out, my way of not listening to my own inner voice.

I often wonder what would have happened had I not had my son, Lucas. He was my turning point, the bringer of light into my life. It was having Lucas that deeply shifted my values. Creating a future that would give him choices was my driver. This gave me an incredible drive to wake up every day and knock on doors and grow my business, with an eight-month-old baby in tow. I started creating a business that would not only make a difference to people's lives, but would pay me enough money to support us both. Being a sole parent is one of the hardest things I've ever done, and the most rewarding.

I'll never forget the night I was curled up in a ball on the floor of my apartment alone, with my little baby asleep next to me. I was swimming in a world of doubt, uncertainty and self-hatred. *How did I get here?* I thought. *This is not my life. How am I supposed to inspire others when I'm so lost and empty? How do I get out of this? I have no income and now I'm a sole parent. I'm trapped.*

I'm not sure how the next moment happened, or what led me to turn my head toward an old box of books I'd had for years. I'd packed them away waiting for the time I could unpack them and put them on the bookshelf.

I moved over to the box, reached in and pulled out a book that a dear friend had given me when I was eighteen. It was a book with quotes on each page. The idea was that you opened it up randomly with an intention in mind and the quote you first saw was your message. I had not done this since I was in my early twenties, when life was so magical to me, so wistful and perfectly synchronistic. That was when I truly believed in the power of living a deeply inspired life, but over the years of disappointment and being let down, I had lost that part of me.

I thought I'd thrown that book away.

I picked up the book, flicked open to a random page and read.

'Crisis events often explode the illusions that anchor our lives.'

In that moment, I had such an epiphany that the illusion I had was my belief about myself. A deeply ingrained belief that I couldn't achieve success because I had a child, because I was a sole parent, because I lived in a town that had not much going on. So I started asking different questions. What if I could create a successful business that allowed me to inspire people, make money, and provide me with enough freedom to care for my son?

I started to think about all the times when I had been able to make things work in my life. Suddenly my mind was recalling great memories of times when I had succeeded or had been able to get my life working. As this movie played out in my mind, I started to feel better inside. I started to feel a deep sense of hope and courage, and that I *could* do this.

Once I had asked a different question, I noticed I started to see my vision much more clearly. I started to visualise what I wanted to create. I could see it in brilliant colour. There I was speaking to people, changing lives and bringing hope, courage and inspiration. In that moment, I made the decision. What if I just 'showed up' every day and was ready for all the opportunities coming my way? I shifted the focus off the illusion of doubt and fear, and moved to a vision of possibility and inspiration. I took action, gained more confidence and started connecting with people, getting out of my comfort zone, reading and absorbing myself in doing things that would help others as much as possible.

The movie in my mind was of me running my own business, training, coaching, facilitating and helping people achieve their goals. I started to see myself working with small groups at first; then I saw the room filled with people. I could see myself talking in front of large groups, inspiring people and making a difference. At this point in my vision, I started to cry and said to myself, *Is this really possible? Can I really have a life that will make my heart sing and make a difference in the world?*

You might be saying to yourself, 'That's all well and good for you, you had contacts, you knew stuff.' Actually, I didn't have a network. When I started, all I had was a vision. Every night, I visualised my business and what I would create. I even made a vision board of what my business would look like over the following twelve-month period. To this day, I create vision boards for my business and visualise the things I want to create. The power of having clarity and a vision is what got me where I am today.

The depth of my certainty during a time that might appear full of uncertainty was what got me through. I took action when I doubted, I made calls when I didn't want to, I went out of my way to meet new people and talk about my business because I knew I needed to do it. It had become a must for me. If I didn't take action, it would be easy to sink into self-doubt and uncertainty, and I knew that the self-doubt was going to be the only thing that would stop me. So I kept moving. Every day I did something, not letting any moments of doubt creep in and take what I had decided to do.

Looking back, I'm not sure how I did it, being a sole parent while starting and building a business. I know I had some family members, an amazing daycare facility and great friends who helped with Lucas, and I wouldn't be here without that support. The most important thing for me was my psychology, keeping my mind 'fit' and focused.

Over ten years on, my first business, Bounce Consulting, a training and coaching business, is going strong, with an incredible team that has been helping inspire people and get them back into employment. With the success of the Bounce Program I could expand into the United States, and now have a company based there. I was even lucky enough to go to the White House for a meeting with its chief technology officer. I have recently started another company, MyAlura, which sells business bags for women, purely from being frustrated about not finding the perfect laptop bag for work.

With the growth of my business also came challenges, disappointments, lies and deception. With all this, I have grown. I listen to my inner voice now, and it is stronger than any other. Perhaps the greatest lesson I have learnt is that there is no failure, just opportunities to learn and grow. I once, for example, had a vision of a new business venture that I thought was going to be incredible, so I invested my team and money into my new vision. However, after eighteen months with no income and money going out, I realised that my business idea was not going anywhere. So I decided to stop the project and admit defeat. At the time, I questioned myself: should I have done something different? How did I miss the signs, where was my inner voice for this one? I wanted to know 'why', what the lesson was, so that I could get it and move on. Sometimes pushing the river just doesn't work. There was no flow, no ease, and that's always been an indicator to me. (That's not to say things that are hard aren't worthy of being created; this is just my thing.) However, it's interesting that as I write this, I realise that had I not done that project I would never have met Danielle, and therefore would not have been asked to write this chapter.

Today my life is full, busy, beautiful and inspired. For the past eight years I have been with an incredibly grounded, loving, kind man who has taken Lucas under his wing and raised him as his own. He also has three beautiful kids who I have helped raise, and with our big family life is busy and full, as well as funny, fun and joyful. Between cricket, basketball, football and school, Lucas has been given the most brilliant opportunity to be raised by a good man and have siblings he never would have had. He has been gifted with wonderful role models who demonstrate how to treat others and how to be kind. I'm so deeply grateful that he has been given this kind of love in his life.

From my years of working with thousands of people from all walks of life, I have realised that my greatest passion is helping people go from being on the floor curled up in a ball, feeling hopeless and helpless and believing their negative thoughts about themselves, to reminding them that those thoughts are not real, but are rather the illusions that anchor them to lives that do not make their heart sing. Helping them listen to their own inner voice, to make the whisper loud and clear within.

When I started running my first business, I found that preparing for the week ahead allowed me to manage the ups and downs of being a mum. Sunday night became my planning and review night.

Pick a night or morning that works for you, and set aside at least twenty minutes. Look at the things you achieved and the things you didn't get to do. Put the things you didn't get to on your to-do list for the week ahead. Focus on what you want to achieve by the end of the week – big chunks, not lots of little ones. This will make things more manageable.

14

Danielle

Obstacles, career changes and brave ideas

Danielle Ross Walls loves her work organising community-focused events. In 2015 she created the first expo for working mothers, Career Ideas for Mums, in Melbourne. Danielle also enjoys freelance writing that is largely travel-focused, with an aim to get people – especially children – engaged in nature, history and related conservation. Her other big loves are her boys and family time firstly, and then, in no particular order, the works of Charles Dickens, Scotland, photographing fungi, passionate people making the world better, reading, animals, collecting vintage Enid Blyton books, Tasmania, dreaming and creating, and her idol, J.K. Rowling.

I was in my early twenties and not long out of university. I was standing on my own in my work staff canteen when he approached me and asked why I didn't wear skirts to work more often. I was taken aback, of course, but his question also left me embarrassed, burning-hot red and speechless. It was a new job that I loved, with a fun, sociable and – ironically – forward-thinking company. He was the CEO. He was a shrewd, wealthy and charismatic entrepreneur. He had a penchant for getting up close in your personal space, and the intimidation was made worse by his remarkable height. I was shy in those days and a bit naïve. That sexist remark was just one of many inappropriate incidents that happened not just to me, but to some of my colleagues, too.

Over twenty years later, I find it liberating to look back and see how far I have come. I'm no longer that shy and naïve. It was a toxic work environment and a horrible experience, but in some small way, a seed was sown for me that day. On some deep level, I had always known that I, too, would turn one of my bold ideas into something like that CEO had done with his business. But that experience made me even more determined to do just that. One day, I would do 'my thing' – without the intimidation – and hopefully, I felt, my ideas might even help others.

Fast-forward to now, and I have had many 'jobs'. I've almost always enjoyed working, but being a mum will always be the best job that I have ever had (and the most challenging). My love for my boys is all-consuming – the fiercest love of all. My other jobs prior to becoming a mother were predominately within the travel and advertising industries. I am now coordinating community-focused events. I also write. I am doing what I love.

It's been a winding road at times, but every glitch along the way has been an integral part of that journey.

When I left the company with the sexist CEO, I ventured into the world of newspaper and magazine advertising, and as time progressed this included online advertising and marketing. I was glad for some transferrable skills, particularly those related to relationship-building. During my fifteen or so years immersed in the fast-paced world of all things advertising, there were several times that I yearned for the missed experience of a 'gap year' in my youth. Twice I took career breaks. (That is to say, I quit my job.) The first time I ventured to Queensland and spent several months on the magical island K'gari/Fraser Island – living in staff accommodation, working in hospitality and partying quite a bit!

Many years later I set off again, on a bigger adventure – a new life in the United Kingdom. Edinburgh first, followed by Northern Ireland. I was an 'older' traveller embarking on a working holiday visa, and in my early thirties. I loved every moment – soaking up the history, learning about my Scottish and European roots, and delighting in the romance of their literary greats. I imagined my hero, J.K. Rowling, writing the Harry Potter books over coffee and cake, as I sat in that same café where she wrote overlooking the magical Edinburgh Castle. I travelled alone again, and did some paid work that was not in my usual field. I had only myself to rely upon, and although I was lonely at times, I felt empowered. In Scotland, I felt that I had come home, but in Belfast I was more out of my comfort zone, as there were few travellers in a similar situation to me. But, in general, my experiences were positive beyond my expectations, and changed me to my core. Challenge now had a different definition.

Not long after I returned to Australia, and returned to an advertising role at a daily newspaper, I met my husband. Ironically, it was through a friend I had made in Belfast. After we had our first child, I knew that my priorities had changed. I did not want to return to the world of advertising once my maternity leave was up. Sure, I'd miss the glamorous and creative parts that I loved, but I didn't feel it would be a family-friendly environment (in the way I needed). I had also decided I wanted a change, to organise events that the community could enjoy – festivals, expos and family days. I knew that my career experience would be valuable as there were some aligned skills, but I was unsure of my next step toward this new career.

So I immersed myself wholeheartedly in an events diploma. Studying part-time was a joy. The combination of classes and online study was perfect. I could enjoy quality time with my then two-year-old, as I only needed to study on campus once a week or fortnight. I soaked it up and was no doubt the annoying mature-age student in class – hand in the air ready to answer any question with enthusiasm!

But this enthusiasm was short-lived. After completing my diploma, I felt stuck. I was in my late thirties looking for an entry-level events job that people half my age were suited to. I wanted a flexible role that would fit in with my family as much as possible. I had such a desire to learn about the industry, but the big problem was my lack of experience. The only event-related experience that I had was organising my own garden wedding, my twenty-year secondary school reunion, and the staff HR Christmas party in Edinburgh. Hardly the makings of a stand-out résumé in the events industry. To make it even harder, I wanted a role that, ideally, would allow me to work from home, because I wanted minimal time away from my son.

Throughout my working life, my roles have involved a high degree of networking. I enjoy making genuine connections with people. I love the win–win that often comes from it. I place a high importance on the skill of networking, so although I felt stuck for experience I threw myself into volunteering for events. It enabled me to extend my professional skills and also allowed me to foster some mutually beneficial connections. This helped me to get references and, on one occasion, my volunteering role turned into a paid position.

The usefulness of this skill was reinforced when a journalist from a newspaper where I had once worked – who also lived in my community – introduced me to some local event contacts, which resulted in a start to my new career. This was the work-from-home role that I desperately wanted. The process of acquiring the position was extremely lengthy, however, and by the time I was offered the role I was pregnant with our second child. A blessing, of course! The hours for the role were minimal, it seemed – maybe ten per week – but it ended up being so much more than part-time.

I gave birth in mid-March, and the event I was organising (a festival) was a mere ten weeks later. I was up at all hours, sleep deprived and absolutely exhausted as a mother to a newborn. I was also dealing with challenging behaviour from my eldest, then four years old – not totally unexpected, of course, as he was adjusting to no longer being the centre of our world.

I was writing and collating marketing material, boosting posts and interacting on Facebook and Twitter, and running purely on adrenaline. Not that I realised it at the time. However, I knew something was wrong when I became so stressed that my breastmilk wouldn't 'let down', despite having had no previous problems. Right then and there, I made myself slow down and allowed myself to relinquish (albeit only slightly) the high standards I had set for myself. I had so desperately wanted my first role in my new career to succeed.

When it had all finished, I consciously stood back and reassessed my priorities for future work. I have no regrets, because that festival experience and the connections I made led to another wonderful community event. During my work on that subsequent event, I felt out of my depth on a few occasions, but a dear friend who had extensive event-management experience, and whom I greatly admire, turned into an invaluable mentor. We chatted endlessly over cups of tea while our children played, and I would pick her brain. Her advice was priceless then, and still is.

By the time my second child turned one, I needed to return to the security of a permanent role rather than the instability of freelance contracts. I came across a part-time role with a corporate organisation in the event space.

My thrill in winning the role was short-lived. I lasted six weeks before I quit – exhausted both physically and mentally. My beautiful baby boy had been introduced to being at childcare (with his older brother), but was frequently sick. If only I had a dollar for every time someone told me that he was 'building up immunity' – likely true, but not helpful at the time. He was breastfeeding at night and I was severely sleep deprived. But I did my very best and in those six weeks managed to juggle his care between my husband and other family members – feeling sick to my stomach at times that I could not be with him.

The demise of this role began the day I arrived at work with a blocked ear. I casually mentioned this to the then-friendly twenty-something colleague sitting beside me. I was shocked to learn that she held built-up frustration toward me. She almost exploded with a retort about being 'sick of training a mum whose children are always sick' and inferred that I should be at home – my blocked ear was not contagious! I can't remember if I was initially speechless or just sobbed at the unfairness of it all. I was trying so hard to be a good mum and trying so hard to be a good employee. So I quit. I was exhausted and overwhelmed and angry and sad.

I stopped paid work and instead enjoyed being a stay-at-home-mum for a while (just as hard as being paid to work in my opinion).

We do not need magic to transform our world. We carry all the power we need inside ourselves already.

– J.K. Rowling

So I kept going, but it had become clear that it was time to bring one of my big ideas to life – to stop dreaming and start doing. For that seed to finally sprout. And to do something I loved that fitted in with my family.

All the time that I had a steady job, I always had a different project or idea playing out in my head. Sometimes, those ideas worked in with my employer – for example, when employed in the advertising industry, I saw a niche and created a new magazine. This time, however, I had only my role as a mother and no other job distraction, and my recent experience had got me thinking – a lot. In some ways, the moment was inevitable.

It was on my fortieth birthday, while watching *Les Misérables* at the Princess Theatre, that my new baby was born. **Suddenly, it all clicked. I knew. I would do an event for mums looking for family-friendly employment options. I'd call it the 'Career Ideas for Mums Expo'.** Oddly enough, I was actually glad (in hindsight), to have experienced discrimination as a working mother – it had propelled me into action.

I am not even sure I heard the beautiful revolutionary chorus of 'Do you hear the people sing?' that day. My mind was elsewhere with thoughts of my new idea. The significance of the song was not lost on me, though. I certainly heard my own voice coming through loud and clear.

Somehow, I had the confidence that resulted in an expo with more than 500 attendees, thirteen speakers and 40 exhibitors. Fortunately, I also had the extra support of my husband, a passionate family daycare educator, the occasional help of a paid assistant, a business coach, an event mentor, and my family and friends. I also had the help of some amazing volunteers on the day of the expo.

I got great media coverage and sponsorship for the event. I really tried to 'think outside the box' and use my previous experience in the advertising industry to help market the event and myself. I obtained my very first sponsor by politely 'crash-tackling' muesli entrepreneur Carolyn Creswell at a council-run breakfast event. When it was post-event photo time, I said hello and then slipped a professionally-bound sponsorship proposal under her arm, much to her surprise! Within two hours, I had an email from her personal assistant with a most generous offer of 1000 Carman's muesli bars for my expo show bags. Other highlights included my first interview on ABC Radio as well as interviews in the *Herald Sun*, parenting magazines and local newspapers. *The Age* ran an article entitled 'Melbourne's first career expo for working mothers'. I felt proud of the exposure – I had worked hard to generate it. Despite making enough money to fund the event through sponsors and ticket sales, it was difficult to pay myself – perhaps not unusual for a first-time event. Still, I have no regrets. I learnt so much – the grassroots event experience, the inherent value of connections, and the deep importance of self-care and not taking on too much. I again realised just how much I loved bringing ideas to life, and gained extra confidence in my own capability and resilience.

The experience led to my current part-time position, a community-focused events role. I also write. My freelance travel writing is mainly around conservation and getting children engaged with nature and history. I have also written stories with my children that we'd love to publish. There is so much that I would love to do, and I have to be careful not to take on too much at once. (I have had to defer my part-time university studies in creative writing to work on my first book-publishing deal – a very exciting project!)

Recently, I organised an event that featured a question-and-answer session. Afterwards, I was talking to the MC about my upcoming publishing deal and disclosed that I may have a case of 'imposter syndrome'. He kindly explained an analogy to me. It suggests that in a Q&A session of approximately one hundred people, of each question the audience asked, there are another eighteen or so people ready with a question, too – they just don't always speak up. He told me that I am the person who grabs that microphone and asks that question. So, I guess that even if at times I might find it hard to believe that I am now a published writer, I at least have the unwavering belief in the fact that I am willing to task risks and put myself out there.

I have always been a dreamer. Like all of us, I am a work in progress – always learning and making mistakes. Sometimes I doubt myself, but I know that the worst that can happen is that I fail. I'd rather that than not try at all.

I've found so many things that light me up. I am so glad to be doing what I love. I think my children have really helped with that – I see the world in a more grassroots kind of way these days. I hope it all rubs off on them and they find what they love. That they too, might one day do *their* thing.

I delight in the glimpses of it.

> I need to rebalance myself with regular time out immersed in nature – no matter the season or weather. It is an integral part of my self-care that allows me to exercise and be surrounded by calm: the sound of silence, birdsong or the ocean. This in itself is my own type of meditation. I feel deep appreciation and a connection to the magic of our environment. As well as being time for myself, I also regularly take my young children with me. We hike and play games hunting for unique types of fungi (Google our favourite, the *Mycena Interrupta*!) in the nearby national parks. Sometimes we play eye-spy or hunt for shells at the beach. They also love to take their own photographs on our adventures.

15

Tiffany

Identity, work and faith

Tiffany Gilmour has dabbled in all things theatre and festivals and currently sings and tells stories for little people. She has two awesome kids, a guinea pig called Nibbles and is a newbie Christian trying to work out what it all means.

I had an identity crisis when I had my first child. I went from a confident, internationally experienced arts worker to a sleep-deprived, domestic milking cow who could no longer shower independently. Before having kids, my husband and I decided to divide and conquer. We would both do part-time work and part-time child raising. An equal division of labour and love. However, as the child raising began, so did the feeding issues, the sleep issues and the accompanying exhaustion. I was dizzy. I had migraines. My GP sent me for blood tests. A brain scan. Counselling. Turns out, I was tired. Just so tired. I stopped driving more than ten minutes at a time, afraid of making a poor judgement call or falling asleep in the car. My husband and I sank into the traditional roles we vowed not to take. He went to work full-time. I stayed home.

The old adage, 'It's not what happens to you but how you deal with it that counts' has been a belief throughout my years as a working mum. My search for meaning, joy and a slowly deepening understanding of faith has punctuated the chapters of my life and informs my life choices in my adult years. As I reflect, I can see that the search widened from home, to school, to city, to continent, to the world and, in many ways, being a working mum has brought that search right back home.

At high school, I was one of five female prefects who were encouraged to do maths at university level. I was accepted into a Bachelor of Engineering. Dad was so proud. He thought I'd build bridges, landmarks, make an impact on the world. I kept telling people I wanted to be an environmental engineer so that I could save penguins from oil spills. Truth was, I didn't really understand what an engineer did and realised that this choice of study had not really been my own. I'd been persuaded to be another female in the 'girls in non-traditional roles' statistics for my high school.

I changed to a different university to study languages. I told everyone I wanted to learn about people and cultures and work for the Department of Foreign Affairs and Trade, but in reality I spent most of my time treading the theatrical boards, sewing costumes and building papier mâché pirate ships. I discovered multilingual theatre and found joy in creating theatre with people from different cultures. We used English, Indonesian and Australian sign language (Auslan) in our performances, receiving critical acclaim and touring Indonesia and London.

As my confidence grew, so did my discontent with Australia, and like many young Aussies, I left for the United Kingdom. In Edinburgh, I grabbed a map of venues of the Edinburgh Festival Fringe and walked, looking for a job. A comedy venue took me in and I found myself managing two theatres from 11 am till 3 am, seven days a week. I lived on a handful of sultanas and two multivitamins per day and had more energy than I've ever had in my life. I cut my teeth in the producing world and discovered adrenaline-soaked happiness.

When the festival ended, I got my happiness fix in London working with an international theatre company who produced and presented dynamic and cutting-edge theatre from all over the world. Through them I facilitated theatre projects with unaccompanied teenage refugees. Theatre arts collided with compassion and meaning, and it felt like the beginning of trust and faith creeping into my career. As the facilitators grappled with the participants' realities of horrific loss, trauma and poverty, we danced, sang, juggled and built puppets, all the while learning how to build trust in each other and the unknown.

My eyes bulged with spectacular sights, my heart pounded with excitement, my veins burst with adrenaline. I loved the stress, hard work, long hours. I was living the dream.

On my thirtieth birthday I woke up with the shuddering realisation that I had to have kids. Up until that second, I had not wanted any. Was my boyfriend father material?

In a dodgy sandwich shop on the Southbank, London, I had fallen in love with my now-husband. Edinburgh-born, this lanky Scotsman had stolen my heart when he ordered beetroot for his salad sandwich in his lilting accent. Any man confident enough to risk beetroot stains on his shirt is worth a chat. A beautiful writer, he told me the funniest stories in 144-character text messages as he rode the night bus home from work.

We left London for Melbourne a few years later to find a quieter, more natural life – the smell of gum leaves, the sound of waves, the relaxed Aussie attitude. It was a return home, to the place I had left in disillusionment, searching for a new promise of meaning and joy. As we settled into Australia, grappling with feeling far away from the rest of the world, my husband stayed at home and wrote plays and opera. I went out and project-managed, directed and produced festivals and theatre. A colleague once told me, 'Make a clear choice about how you introduce yourself and your work. You will become that person.' We were reinventing ourselves, trying to trust our decision to return to Australia and find meaning in a world where Mother Nature felt closer. We strolled the beach each morning with cups of tea in hand and pondered where our lives were headed.

And then we had kids. Two of them. The most beautiful, precious, lovable beings I've ever met. Having kids has been the best thing that has happened to me. Ever.

When my first child was one year old, I curated an exhibition of Greek migrant stories. A Greek grandmother befriended my son and took him for walks so I could do interviews. This was a great introduction to a supported working-mum life. A friend once said, 'There are no companies, only people' and this rings true for me. People and personalities can often make or break a working mum's life.

When my second child was about a year old, I began working part-time for our local library; telling stories, singing songs and role-modelling active literacy for toddlers and their carers. But mostly jumping around like a twit. I also use The University of

Melbourne's Abecedarian Approach for early-years literacy with families recently arrived in Australia. I feel positive about my work because research shows that daily reading, singing and talking to your child can improve outcomes in reading and writing and have lasting effects on wellbeing in adult life. Plus I get to sing. Who knew *Incy Wincy Spider* could change a life?

The thing about working at the library was that, on the one hand, I was loving entertaining and educating families, but on the other, I felt guilty about swanning off to work on a Saturday morning, leaving my hubby with screaming children who missed their mum and were not used to being looked after by Dad. The guilt of enjoying work and time away from my kids was confronting. The relief and pleasure at having my own income again was freeing.

Ask a working mum how they are and they'll often talk about mother guilt, baby brain, and the insanity of juggling overcommitted, busy lives. With young kids, I had half-conversations with friends: 'I had this amazing ... (pause to catch runaway child) ... opportunity to do a ... (pause to take random sharp object out of child's mouth) ... sorry, I have to change his nappy now.' Ugh. A friend said to me that she honestly questioned her ability to hold a proper conversation any more. Baby brain feels like it can last for years, and the guilt feels like it will last a lifetime. We rarely left our kids in childcare, preferring to nurture them at home and not wanting to deal with the childcare mum-guilt issue and finding it costly anyway. I've been lucky to be able to work during kinder hours, at night or on the weekend when my hubby could look after the kids.

For a whole year, every Saturday after storytelling at the library,

I walked past the local Church of Christ. One time, the church was advertising a craft market. Now I like a bit of country craft, a bit of pink gingham, and thought I'd like to pop in. On the day of the market, I got home from work, and hubby and I had a doozy of an argument. Unusually, I then went for a walk to calm down and headed to the craft market. The official welcomer, Liz, put me at ease with her vivacious no-nonsense style of down-to-earth chatter, until she said: 'I'll introduce you to the minister.'

'Please don't disturb him,' I said, my comfort draining away.

But then I met her. Minister Megan. She was, like, 30 years old. Female. And normal.

Megan invited me for coffee and we started meeting regularly. She taught me about Jesus and I discovered that the clues I'd been uncovering all my life, the meaning I'd been searching for, were pointing to Him. From an early age I've been looking for something; for faith, for meaning, for God. I have memories from age five onwards of moments alluding to a spiritual world. I dabbled in Buddhism, Sufism, angel cards and the like, magpieing the bits I liked. I didn't grow up in a religious family. We never went to church. But growing up I had learnt about kindness, joy, gentleness, fortitude and resilience, qualities I believe to be generated by faith.

My work and faith have begun to merge as I now work a second part-time job as the office administrator at our local Church of Christ. The job could ultimately be an admin job in any venue, just with extra lovely people, but it's not. It's an outward expression of who I am at the moment. More and more I'm beginning to explore how faith influences my work and family life. The way I talk, how I carry out my work, the quality of my interactions, my choices and the way I mother my kids. Never in a million years would I have guessed that in my forties my work would define me as a Christian. My faith no longer exists as something private and personal; it has become public and part of a community. And it's a fantastic job to boot. I'm literally working out and living out how to be a mum, how to work, and how to have faith through it all.

I love that my paid work allows me the freedom and flexibility to be present with my kids to enjoy the everyday with them. I'm one of those mums who loves school holidays. I'm happiest when the kids and I are home just pottering about, doing everyday life together and alongside each other; sharing, learning, laughing, playing. My kids and my faith have taught me to look with fresh eyes at the world from two feet high. Beetles, snails, sticks, stones, water. Such miraculous nature around us and it's so easy to miss it. My children have taught me to do things more slowly. Is it really necessary to rush *all the time*? Do I really have to finish that ever-so-important to-do list? Is clean enough, good enough? In contrast, my children have also enabled me to work more swiftly. I can now get done in two hours what used to take me a whole day. My faith and my kids are teaching me to be present rather than perfect, and in doing so they are also helping me to reprioritise both my daily tasks and my future career path.

Our journey as a young family has had significant times of challenge, darkness, anxiety and illness, and while time is a great healer, so are supportive mum-friends, family, friends, neighbours, new-dads' groups, community and workplaces. Eight years on, I am no longer in crisis mode; I'm in invention mode. My goal is that my future work will be family-friendly and will combine my love of cultures, the arts and my faith. I'm not sure what that will be. I'm holding a pen and a blank book, eager to write the next chapter and be guided by my faith. What do I want? Who am I now? Who does God want me to be?

> Read three books to your child each day from birth to five years and you will expose them to around 10,000 words by the time they start school. Sure, you might have to read their favourite book a thousand times, but the rich language and ideas you will introduce your child to, plus the quality time of snuggling together on a couch, will go a long way in building a love of learning. It doesn't matter what you read. Read the newspaper or a magazine if you want – just read. It will give them a huge head start in literacy and lifelong wellbeing.

16

Aleisha

Taking the leap: starting a clinic from home

Aleisha Rasheed is a doctor of Chinese medicine and owner of Altona Acupuncture, a clinic she established to provide high-quality healthcare solutions and ensure that her clients' first approach to illness or pain is a natural one. Aleisha holds degrees in Chinese medicine and human biology, undertook a clinical internship at Nanjing Jiangsu Provincial Hospital in China, and is undertaking a Master of Human Nutrition.

I always had a gut feeling that I would have twins, so when I fell pregnant with a singleton baby, I was a little surprised. It didn't match the plans I had made in my head. Get married, finish uni at 30, have twins (thereby knocking off the need to get pregnant again, as I wanted two children), spend a year at home breastfeeding and cooking meals from scratch before launching my career as an acupuncturist and running a successful clinic by the time the kids were in school. Easy.

I didn't realise how arrogant those plans were until I was eight weeks pregnant and noticed that I was spotting. Even though Dr Google told me spotting in the first trimester was normal, my husband rushed me to the hospital. The nurses also told me that it was normal so I felt assured that everything would be okay, but they sent me for an ultrasound anyway.

The sonographer stared at the screen and barely glanced my way as she told me that the shape of the embryo was irregular, denoting that I had miscarried. I don't know if she was emotionless as a protective mechanism or if she was just so used to seeing this type of thing, but I remember that it felt inappropriate to cry in front of her. I guess it can't be an easy job. I don't think I exhaled once while she was in the room.

When she closed the door behind her, I lost control and cried so hard. I was in so much pain.

My husband was optimistic and just wanted to try again straight away. The way he dealt with the miscarriage was completely different to me. He saw it as a speed bump and wanted to get pregnant again as soon as possible. In my eyes, I didn't lose an embryo, I lost my child. Before the dilatation and curettage (D&C), I slowly bled out for two weeks, passing debris every day, knowing that at any moment I could have a massive gush and intense pain as the pregnancy terminated itself completely. The whole process felt traumatic, and I felt alienated from my husband and my friends who felt obliged to offer advice after the miscarriage, which generally made me feel worse. I already felt so much guilt and disappointment in my body, as if it had somehow let me down and failed my husband.

I didn't try to get pregnant again right away. I went to China for two months to finish my five-year Chinese medicine degree with an internship at a hospital in Nanjing. It was one of the most amazing experiences of my life. China was the first country I have visited where I felt a real culture shock and I loved it. I loved seeing the way the Chinese use Chinese medicine in the context of their culture. The hospitals were definitely not like home, with ten to twenty people crammed into a tiny office as the ailing patient presented intimate details about their medical history to the doctor in front of complete strangers.

The Chinese thought I was absolutely bizarre, a giant yellow-haired woman that they would approach with curiosity to take selfies with, usually without asking. When my girlfriend and I would jog through the city, people would drop everything and stare at us as if we were escaped giraffes galloping through the city streets. I really loved the little things, like seeing couples in matching clothes walking hand in hand through the middle of the city. I loved riding my bike through Nanjing under the huge maple trees that lined the streets. China cleared my soul of shame and hurt, and when I got back to Australia my husband and I tried to get pregnant immediately.

When I peed on the stick this time, the double lines were so dark there was absolutely no doubt that I was pregnant. We visited the GP and requested an eight-week ultrasound. This time, the sonographer was extremely chirpy and slightly goofy. He instructed me to lie down so that he could see if there were one or two babies inside me. **My husband and I laughed. The sonographer covered my belly with jelly and began the ultrasound and two little embryos appeared on the screen.** 'See, I told you and you didn't believe me,' the sonographer quipped before taking a phone call … yes, he took a personal call during the ultrasound. I looked at my husband and his hands were covering his gaping mouth, his eyes were wide and he started laughing. We were so happy and felt so blessed.

The pregnancy, however, was horrendous. I was huge immediately and in a maternity bra by the end of the eighth week. I remember bumping into a girl from high school who was about 36 weeks pregnant. When I told her I was twenty weeks, she looked at my stomach sympathetically and said, 'Ooh, you still have a long way to go.' I had a few occasions of vomiting in public and a few near misses. I crawled into bed immediately after work and felt chronically ill for the entire nine months ... but I still felt so blessed.

My girls were delivered at 37 weeks and five days and weighed 2.79 kilograms and 2.84 kilograms, which is big for twins but still so tiny. I was so lucky and I felt a surge of intoxicating love as soon as I laid eyes on them.

The first night was a blur, but I know that they cried non-stop. It wasn't long until I realised that I was not producing enough milk. The girls were small and born with jaundice, so they needed to be fed every three hours. I decided to supplement with formula until my milk came in. I had expected to be one of 'those mums' who hold one twin in each arm and tandem feed. I had pictured myself doing it throughout the pregnancy and read so much literature about how to make it work, but my supply was just so low and eventually one of my girls just wouldn't latch any more. I thought my supply was improving until I visited the breastfeeding service at the hospital and was told that I should have been producing 2 litres of milk per day by now. It was at that point that I realised that my body was failing me again. Not just me but my kids, too. I was told that to build supply, I needed to breastfeed each baby for one hour (30 minutes on each breast) followed by 30 minutes of expressing on each breast afterwards. That meant I would need to be feeding for three out of every four hours.

A dark cloud descended over me. I just couldn't do it. The guilt and shame I felt at being unable to breastfeed is something that I carry with me until this day. The sad thing is that if I had the clinical experience I have now as a Chinese herbalist, I would know exactly which herbs to take to help build my supply. I can make all the excuses I want, but at the end of the day it is a shame that I will probably feel for the rest of my life.

They say that breastfeeding is the way to bond with your child, but let me assure you that being unable to breastfeed did not impact my connection with my daughters one little bit. The first ten months of their lives was the most special time in my life. But after that, something changed. The sleepless nights started to take their toll, and the girls started crawling. It is so strange how one little change can make life a thousand times more difficult. By the time they were twelve months old, I was desperate to get to work and have some time to myself. I started working one day a week in a clinic a couple of suburbs away. The drive on my first day of work was awesome. I was smiling like a crazy person, playing music loud and singing 'Ice Cube' at the top of my lungs. Working gave me the respite I needed to recharge my battery and learn to function as a normal human in society again.

I don't know what it is about being a parent – perhaps it's the weekends spent doing family-rated activities rather than partying – but I decided that along with work, I should go back to uni and do a Master of Human Nutrition. And because I had so much free time on my hands, I also decided to start a community group to lobby the council to establish a community garden in my suburb. I started my Masters doing a full-time course load of three subjects over the trimester. I also formed a committee for the community group, and we grew the membership to around eighty people, became incorporated, and presented a proposal for a community garden to council. No biggie.

I wasn't diagnosed, but I think I might have had a nervous breakdown. Every night I dreamt that waves were crashing over me as I desperately tried to keep my head above water. One day the local newspaper was coming over to take a photo of my daughters and me in front of our veggie patch, to report on the work I was doing to establish the community garden. Thirty minutes before the photographer came, the girls were screaming and throwing tantrums. (Something that happens in tandem when you have twins.) It all got too much and I broke down and cried, sobbing loudly with my head in my hands as my girls watched me, horrified. I always swore I would never cry in front of my kids – just another thing to add to the growing list of things I swore I would never do. The photographer came and took the photo of us and it filled half a page in the local paper. My face looked as if I just had an allergic reaction to a bee sting.

I knew that I had to focus on the things that are the most important to me – my family and friends and my job that I love. I needed to be present with my daughters in order to enjoy life and I needed to focus on my work because it fulfils me and supports our family.

I finished the first trimester of my Masters and stepped down from my role as president of the community group. The night I stepped down, I went to sleep with a smile on my face and had a dream that I was walking topless in a calm and quiet swimming pool made of marble. I was the only person there and the water only came up to my waist. It was lovely.

At the end of 2016, I decided to take the leap and start my own acupuncture clinic from home. Things are going well and my business is growing, but I know what my limits are and where I can push myself. Being a mum has made me challenge myself more in the last four years than I ever have before.

> Your experience is unique, so don't compare yourself to other mums. You never know what another mum is going through, no matter how perfect or flawed she may seem from the outside.

17

Chloe

Early childhood educator challenges senator on social media

Chloe Chant is an early childhood education and care (ECEC) professional whose profile skyrocketed after she wrote an open letter to an Australian senator. The letter, which went viral, was her eloquent and insightful response to the senator's controversial public comments on the value of the work done by ECEC professionals.

I came to the early childhood education and care (ECEC) sector after having my own child. My naïve and idealistic thought process went something like this: *I'm not bad at looking after kids ... this will be easy ... it's a sector full of women with children ... they'll understand!* But as the winter sun disappears, I now find myself anxiously counting children and calculating ratios so that I can maybe leave at 5.30 pm, even though my shift ended at 5 pm. I'm hoping I might be able to pick up my own child from her service before it closes. I watch each parent arrive, hug their child, pack up bags and head off for the night. On nights when I can't legally leave due to the time parents are picking up their children, I make desperate calls to my husband or friends so that my own child isn't left waiting at the front door at 6 pm – with an invoice for late pick-up. It's at times like these that I really appreciate the gap many women feel between 'idealistic thought processes' and the reality we face as working mums.

It's a gap I feel acutely as an early childhood educator. One of the things I find hardest to do is reassure women that I understand how they feel. It is regrettable when either party – mother or educator – feels that they are not in this complex business of nurturing children and coping with modern life together. How many times have I read into the anguished faces of mothers dropping off their kids simple but pressing emotional questions like, 'Do they love me enough?', 'Do I spend enough time with them?', 'Why do they cry when I drop them off?', 'Why *don't* they cry when I drop them off?', 'Why are they cuddling their teacher so tight? Hang on, did they just call her mummy?!'

It's hard when a gulf opens up between educators and mothers who feel guilty about 'leaving their children behind' to be cared for and nurtured by another. Everyone knows this guilt is unreasonable, but it is also understandable. It seems to me a stronger relationship between parents and educators is only possible when it is recognised that the full cultural reality of parent identity in the 21st century involves women establishing a viable connection between the world of work and the world of motherhood.

I understand the feelings, because I have them myself, but I also recognise the reality. As an educator, I am no less subject to the pangs of guilt that mothers feel in these circumstances, but I also feel proud that I can help women like me to fulfil a set of complex, ultimately rewarding aspirations. If it takes a village to raise a child, I'm part of that village. I console myself with that thought when I am missing my own child at 6 o'clock on a cold evening as the sun goes down. And I have faith enough in the partnership between me and other parents to feel they, too, can appreciate what I'm doing with (and for) them.

The irony doesn't escape me. I work in a sector that bourgeoned in the 1970s because it became increasingly necessary to support women who wanted to be part of the workforce. It's 2017 now, and I want to be part of the workforce too, but the very industry that has historically supported women who want control over their economic destiny barely pays me enough to make it a viable option. Advances in neuroscience have now clearly shown us that quality early education in the first five years of life is critically linked to future success. Regardless of the need for 'child-minding', such an experience is the right of children everywhere – that is, of course, if you believe in equality of opportunity. However, there are some who still view this as 'women's work' and, as such, figure that the remuneration should be either minimal or non-existent. When you look at male-dominated sectors that require similar levels of qualification, the workers are paid on average about 30 per cent more than a childcare educator. I'm literally earning less as an educator working under professional frameworks than I would as a cleaner of my centre. And so it is, ironically, almost 'not worth it' for me to be a working mum because of the cost of putting my own child into care.

The kind of public commentary, in which some Australian politicians have engaged, that advocates for low-rent, cut-price, rack 'em and stack 'em childcare is not only short-sighted at the national economic level, but also offensive to women working in this industry. As redolent as it is of the sort of 'child-minding' we witnessed in Romanian orphanages during the Balkan conflicts of the past, this sort of childcare has been seriously suggested as the bottom-line option in a model of Australian 'choice', in which some families can elect for more prestigious services … if they can afford it. Can we really risk perpetuating intergenerational poverty and disadvantage by running a two-tier system of early learning and childcare like this? Does such a cynical system of 'choice' really offer any sort of choice at all for the majority of cash-strapped Australian families? Such heartless political agitation that cares nothing for the interests of children or the women who work with them – that prioritises cheap votes over social responsibility – is infuriating.

In January 2017, it made me very mad indeed.

My fifteen minutes of fame began on a quiet Wednesday night. I came home from work exhausted. I did the usual stuff – made dinner, bathed my daughter, read to her, put her to bed, put some washing on and finally slumped down in front of the TV. Unfortunately, my husband beat me to the remote control and so, according to the unwritten household rule that 'whoever turns on the TV gets to pick the show', I was condemned to watching yet another cricket match. As a frazzled and decidedly unsporty person of the non-bloke persuasion, the prospect of several hours of inscrutable competition between teams from Brisbane and Perth left me unenthused, to say the least.

So instead I opened my laptop. I had some vague recollection of colleagues at work chatting about a senator who'd made comments on the early childhood education and care sector, to the effect that it was all a matter of 'wiping noses', preventing kids from 'killing each other' and 'keeping paedophiles from the door'. I did some googling. My husband watched in amusement as my face reddened and my outbursts became less and less child-friendly. I watched clips, read comments, and generally updated myself on what purported to be the prevailing popular opinion about my career. As usual, it seemed to make no difference that those expressing this opinion had no expertise or insight whatsoever into ECEC.

Not without a fight, I thought. Where did this senator get off trivialising the importance of my job and the sector as a whole? How could a supposedly intelligent, enlightened representative of the people wallow in such spectacular ignorance? How could he expect the Australian voting public to join him in the process? I wondered if the apocalyptic, post-truth, 'alternative fact' la-la land we have all been fearing had come to pass. Maybe a person's celebrity or their lucky election in a questionable upper house voting procedure really did entitle them to disregard the wisdom of experts, the knowledge of people who had dedicated their professional lives to an issue as crucial as early childhood education. While this man was busy concocting the sort of populist drivel he believed might get him re-elected, had he not seen the clear example of progressive countries now reaping the rewards of free or appropriately subsidised early childhood education?

So I wrote. My intense anger and disdain 'exploded' onto the screen. I posted an open letter onto my own Facebook page. I wasn't confident of getting much by way of a meaningful response from the senator but, to be honest, my words were intended to be more of an homage to my fellow educators. Provocation of the good senator was not really the primary objective. I suppose it was also a bit cathartic.

> Dear Senator Leyonhjelm,
> Three weeks ago, I stopped everything and spent an entire day of my personal, unpaid time creating documents to be used in court for a family in the middle of a child custody hearing …
> … The next day I went to work and wiped a lot of noses.
> Two weeks ago, I identified behaviours that indicated possible child sexual abuse. I talked to the child, I talked to parents, I consulted research and theory, I completed mandatory reporting requirements, I cried – a lot …
> And I managed to stop the children killing each other.
> This week I held a baby as he experienced febrile convulsions. I cooled him, reassured him, called an ambulance, called the mother, comforted the hysterical mother, evacuated the other children, kept airways open. I provided first aid that could have prevented brain damage or death. I spent four hours filling out legal documentation, paperwork, reflections and analysis.
> … And I wiped some noses.
> On Monday, I completed a set of observations, learning summaries and analyses that culminated in a recommendation that a child be assessed for learning delay. I sat there sweating and feeling nauseated while waiting for the parents to arrive for a meeting to discuss this. I was yelled at, screamed at, accused of being an insensitive, unprofessional bitch and then they cried, and then I hugged them, and then I talked them through all the support and strategy I was going to offer to help them and their child.
> … And, to my knowledge, I managed to let zero paedophiles into my service.

On Wednesday, I said goodbye to a family who were moving on from our service. They thanked me for the support, the documentation, the planning, the individual observations, the learning analyses, the patience, the help in times of crisis, the emotional investment and countless episodes of first-aid treatments in times of emergency.

... *And I wiped some noses.*
... *And changed nappies.*
... *And set up experiences.*
... *And prepared lunches.*
... *And mopped floors.*
... *And mediated conflicts.*
... *And attended staff meetings.*
... *And managed resources.*
... *And taught self-help skills.*
... *And helped children with toilet training.*
... *And was spewed on by babies.*
... *And cleaned up vomit.*
... *And raked the garden.*
... *And helped multiple babies sleep.*
... *And taught pre-literacy skills.*
... *And expanded the vocabularies of the children.*
... *And introduced the concept of nuclear fission.*
... *And explained the fundamentals of DNA.*
... *And explained where babies come from.*
... *And described the purpose of the dendrites on nerve cells.*
... *And I wiped more noses.*
That was Wednesday.
I did this for just over 20 bucks an hour.
Your ignorance regarding the lifelong benefits of early learning

(sorry, a 'middle-class perk' – Leyonhjelm July 2, 2015), arrogance, self-righteousness and hypocrisy as a self-proclaimed champion of enlightened government investment would be hilarious if it wasn't so damaging to our future prospects as an intelligent nation, and the aspirations of the working class.

Should you need any advice regarding the real responsibilities of a childcare worker – or should you need your nappy changed – I am only too happy to render assistance. Despite your comments, my role is to educate, and nothing would please me more than to educate one of my esteemed parliamentary representatives.

During the night I heard my phone beeping with Facebook alerts. I grumpily turned the sound off and tried to settle back down to sleep. The next morning, I rolled out of bed and prepared myself mentally for another difficult day at work managing the transitions, orientations and new enrolments that characterise January at an early learning centre. My husband, who notoriously loves his sleep, was already bolt upright with the laptop in front of him, ready to barrage me with statistics and strategies with a level of excitement on his face that I don't even think I saw on our wedding day. I brushed it off, drove to work, and quickly checked my phone before going 'on the floor'. A journalist had messaged me and asked my permission to attempt to get my letter published on 'Women's Agenda'. Of course! Why not? Oh, you need a photo? Okay, let me scroll back through three years of failed selfies to find a photo that doesn't portray me as a sweaty, slightly overweight, harassed mum who hasn't bought a nice outfit in years.

The experience continued to spiral. I knew the momentum would eventually die, so I just said yes to whatever was offered to me. Being interviewed for radio was just survivable, but appearing live on ABC News 24 left me dangerously close to what we in the industry refer to as 'Code Brown'. It was hard, and I was nervous, and this isn't what I am good at, but the words are out there now, with a life of their own.

Climbing the career ladder of early childhood education sometimes feels more like treading water. In a sector that's yet to be fully professionalised, it's a matter of seizing hold of haphazard opportunities to assume additional responsibility. Okay, I hear you say, you chose this path. So lean in! Well, I frantically train up, attend networking events, lean in mentally and physically so far that I cringe a bit, and every so often feel guilty that I am leaning myself out of my own family responsibilities. At some point in this ridiculous see-saw scenario, I fall face first into 'no-woman's land' and feel despondent, ashamed and unfocused.

At times like these, all I can do is remember my own beautiful mum. She was a stay-at-home mum for about ten years during the time my two siblings and I grew up and went off to 'big school'. Before Mum went to work, I was so proud of her. She was always there to drop me off and pick me up from kindergarten. She had hot chocolate waiting for me on a cold afternoon after piano lessons. She cleaned up my room while I was at school. She went shopping during the day and picked up little treats like a new set of pyjamas or some cool hair ties. Every afternoon I could cuddle up to her in front of the TV, or rely on her to mediate the inevitable conflicts between my sister and me.

However, economic reality obtruded. It soon became apparent that Mum would have to get a job. (Well, a paid job.) I could tell she didn't want to because of her nervousness as she went to interviews and the sadness in her eyes when she dropped us off at before-school care. But I grew to be proud of my mum in a whole new way as she added an extra dimension to her personality. She was more exhausted, but also more and more beautiful. It wasn't just the nice shirts and lipstick she was wearing but, I believe, the pride she radiated as a result of self-determination and professional achievement. Her little girl picked up on that … as all little kids do.

I have taken solace in the history of my mother at every stage of my post-baby life. During maternity leave, during periods of study, during part-time and sometimes full-time employment, I have remembered her story and treasured it. Whatever I'm doing, I hope my little girls are looking up to me now the same way I looked up to my mum when I was their age.

Faith in the confidence and competence of women – it's transmissible. It just needs a habit of mutual support and occasional recognition from those who benefit most from what we continue to do.

> My husband and I have specialised in tasks so that neither of us has to complete cleaning tasks that we absolutely hate. For example, I never touch the dishwashing, but I have sole responsibility for clothes washing.

18

Irene

Twenty lessons about business and life
from an entrepreneur

Irene Falcone is the founder of Nourished Life, a store that provides sustainable, eco-friendly and natural personal care, beauty and lifestyle products. She is a mother of four and winner of the 2016 Telstra Business Women's NSW Entrepreneur Award.

I've always been obsessed with beauty. I love trying new products, seeing the beautiful packaging on my dresser, and that indescribable feeling you get when you leave the house looking all glammed up.

Something that had consumed me almost as much as beauty, however, was fatigue. For years prior to starting my business, I'd accepted it as a normal feeling. I felt heavy and sluggish, but I didn't think the way I felt was unusual. I was a mum, a wife, and I was working in a high-powered corporate job – of *course* I was tired! I had been working in corporate for a decade, seven years of which I had spent in management positions. As you can probably imagine, this required a lot of early mornings and late nights.

I was truly exhausted. I had a husband, two children and two stepchildren, all of whom I barely saw. I'd come to accept this fatigue as normal. But when I found myself really struggling just to make it up a flight of stairs to get to my office, I realised I needed to make a change. I had to physically sit down to catch my breath! While I was sitting on the stairs I thought I might as well apply some body lotion to my legs. I began wondering, *'What's really in this?'* This prompted me to start looking closely at what I was putting onto my skin, and begin my search for effective, natural products.

In 2011, I decided to do a Facebook page and a blog about my journey replacing my makeup products with natural ones. I remember saying to my husband, 'If I can get 100 followers I'll keep doing this as a hobby.' In the first week, I got 1000 followers. I had made the switch to these products to help myself, but when I saw that there were so many others looking for the same things as me, I realised there was something more I could do to help. So, in 2012, Nourished Life was born.

Starting a business was a real risk, even more so because I had absolutely no investment. **I had $100 with which to start the business, and my mother was working for me for free packing orders and doing post office runs – two working mums under the one roof!** With that $100, I bought 100 lip products from the United States and sold them through my blog and my Facebook page. We had maybe five different products back then – now we sell somewhere between 3000 and 4000.

It's been an amazing journey, and one in which I've learnt a lot about running a business as a mum. This includes the following 20 lessons that I hope might also help other mothers who are looking to start, or are already running, their own businesses:

1. Forget balance
When you start a business, the concept of a work–life balance becomes a bit irrelevant. If running your own business means less time with the kids or spending time on the computer on weekends, don't feel guilty. Acknowledge that you can't do everything and that your business is part of your life.

2. Home food delivery is your best friend
The less time you spend cooking, the more time you'll have to actually spend time with your family at home. It's a small sacrifice to make in the scheme of things, although if you're lucky, your partner might cook for you and the kids instead.

3. Fake it until you make it
Never has a truer phrase been spoken. Step into the businessperson role even when you don't feel like you've got the confidence. When I was working from home, I always made an effort to dress nicely for a Skype meeting, and ensured that I came across in whatever I was doing as professional and confident in my actions.

4. Ask for help
If you need help with looking after the kids or household upkeep, don't be afraid to ask friends and family to lend a hand. More often than not, they'll be more than willing to help you out in any way they can. But don't forget to thank them!

5. Find a mentor

Seek out someone whose business or skills you admire, and don't be shy. Approach them, ask for advice, and refer back to them whenever you feel lost or unsure. They can give you guidance and direction during times of uncertainty.

6. Be forward

Too many times I have kept or have seen someone keep quiet about something important. If you disagree with something, question it, and if you want something in particular, make it known so that there's no confusion whatsoever.

7. Look for personality, not experience

When hiring staff, it's about a finding a good fit for your team and ensuring that every team member is passionate about your business and working together. No matter how great someone's CV looks, their personality might not always mesh well with your existing work culture.

8. Get the tough stuff under control

Finding a good accountant, lawyer and bookkeeper is not negotiable. Make sure you've got the right kind of help and ensure they understand your needs exactly.

9. Do what you do best and outsource the rest

Don't concentrate on the areas you're not an expert in. Hire help with the tricky stuff and leave the complicated work to those with the right skills so that you can focus on your own strengths.

10. Embrace your mistakes
If you make a risky decision and it doesn't turn out, learn from it and plan ahead for the future. Turn your errors into strengths by finding out what works and what doesn't.

11. If there's a crisis, deal with it
Crises often threaten to break us, especially when we feel like we can't handle one more thing going wrong, but always figure out a straightforward solution instead of dwelling on it. Ring someone, find a resolution and fix the situation. There is always a way out and it won't be a problem forever.

12. Get a good support network
It's so important to build both internal and external support networks. You need to surround yourself with people you can cry on and laugh with. This includes both your team and your family and friends – you need to be able to trust them and talk to them.

13. Listen to your customers
No matter what kind of customers you have, they can teach you so many things about your own business and give you all kinds of clues as to what to do next or which is the right direction. Often they'll surprise you with some kind of insight you never would have considered yourself.

14. Use social media to your advantage
Get your business on Facebook and Instagram so you can communicate directly with your customers and establish new connections. Make your brand visible and easy to find.

15. Keep it simple

In small business, you'll be approached by various salespeople trying to sell you the latest and greatest software and technologies. While these can be great opportunities, it's important to not feel like you're missing out if you pass them up. You don't always need a new tool or app for everything. Don't overcomplicate things – just pick a couple of key systems to use and say no to the rest.

16. Invest in your people

No matter how good you think you are, your team is your best asset. Invest in teaching them new skills, and learn from them yourself.

17. Don't forget time for you

Sometimes you really do need to help yourself first. Whether you need to take a step back or disconnect completely for a while, it's always a good idea to take a short break if things are getting too much. If you give your mind a chance to refresh and recharge, you'll be better off in the long run and will come back feeling more creative and productive.

18. Don't forget to eat

It might sound silly, but when you're all over the place trying to run a business, it can actually be very easy to forget about putting food in your stomach. If you're like this, don't let it get to the point where you feel like you're about to faint. Whatever you're doing, it can wait for you to take a bite of lunch so that you can actually keep going.

19. Don't underestimate the power of a business plan
Even if you don't stick to it – and often you won't – give yourself some direction and something to fall back on. Having some kind of plan is better than improvising all the time, and you'll feel all the more organised for it.

20. Always follow your gut
Your brain is logical, and your heart is illogical, but your gut always knows. Trust your instincts and go with whatever you feel is right.

These are just some of the lessons I've learnt on this amazing journey, and I look forward to continuing to learn and grow as I continue along it.

> I like to set simple chores for each of the children that they can tick off as they are completed, in return for TV and computer game time.

19

SHARI AND LANA

Sister support

Shari Willis and Lana Walsh are sisters who enjoy an extremely strong bond and who have truly supported each other through the ups and downs of their respective parenting, work and personal journeys. Shari first became a mum at 24 and went on to be blessed with two more beautiful children. She ran a busy retail business while raising three children under four. She is now 42 and has three amazing teenagers. Lana is a single mother of two incredible children who, when not planning her next adventure, is balancing a corporate career. Lana firmly believes that we can achieve our heart's desires if we grow together.

You may be as different as the sun and the moon, but the same blood flows through both your hearts. You need her, as much as she needs you.
— George R.R. Martin

Different! That is the word that comes to mind when I think about Lana (my beautiful sister) and myself. It's funny that two sisters can be brought up under the same roof, with the same parents, and yet be so different. We are six years apart in age, our bodies are shaped differently, we do not look similar at all, our skin colour is opposite and we do not even eat the same way. We have different ideas about parenting, working and money. We even deal with conflict in the most opposite of ways. Lana is always calm, happy and keeping the peace, while I cannot sit still, like to be loud, and am uncomfortable if I am not in constant motion. When we were growing up, you could find Lana chilling watching TV and me off chasing boys. You would think this pattern of behaviour would transfer through to the rest of our lives, but there is one exception and that is in our social lives. Lana is the socialite who must meet up with her friends as often as possible, and I live in a small town and go weeks without meeting up with any of my friends.

How different yet how close can two sisters be?

In December 1999, I had my first beautiful child, and one year later I moved my new little family 150 kilometres away to a new town and a new business. My husband at the time and I were in deep with a retail business and new baby, and we were away from family. I officially worked in this business part-time, but when it's your own it's really full-time.

Eighteen months later our second baby arrived and our business was going strong. I was fairly isolated this whole time, with Lana on the end of the phone but living her younger, fun, partying life. Then we had our third child. By then, life was very busy juggling another new baby, two toddlers and a thriving business. In 2011, my world fell apart. My husband was gone, and with the end of our relationship my business went too.

That was the time when sister power came through for me in full force. My children were eight, ten and twelve. I had no real career skills, but what I did have was determination and the full support of my amazing sister. Lana was working full-time herself, but in any way she could possibly support me, she did. This was a crazy time for me. Lana was there to help me move house six times – yes, six times. You can only imagine the financial stress and juggling act that was my life at this point. What stands out the most is my sister's ability to listen to me cry and vent, with no judgement ever given – just a kind ear, open arms and an open heart.

The other huge shift in my life at that time was the search for myself and my perfect career. I had gone from working at banks to house-cleaning to studying, but have now finally arrived at my dream career as a timeline therapist, self-empowerment coach and nutritional cleansing coach. Wow, what a ride, and all the time with the most supporting, loving and gentle woman I know standing by me. Always believing in me and knowing I would find my way.

Lana brings such balance to my world. About five years ago, she thought it was a great idea, along with our sister-in-law, to put $10 each a week into a joint bank account, and in the future we would know when to use it. I like to be in 'control' of my money, and was unsure if this was the best choice for me, but Lana has proved me wrong many times. With this money, we have since been able to share many super fun trips, and I have been able to finally move away from my tendency to stay with routine, and instead let my hair down occasionally (far from natural for me).

Life now is incredible. I have a brand new husband, three well-adjusted teenage children, an amazing career and a best friend and sister who unconditionally loves and supports me.

And now to Lana's story – but with me still writing, because that is what I do as the big sister. Plus, my little sister is a very busy lady, so, just as she has done for me so many times, I help her whenever and however I can.

While I was busy having babies and building a business, Lana was busy having fun, going on adventures and working (but most of all – let's be honest – partying). While studying her higher school certificate (HSC) she decided that she needed a break from the stress of it all. She moved to Albury to study a tourism course. This led to her moving to Fraser Island, where she had an amazing experience working at a resort and really enjoying the island life of meeting tourists, parties and, of course, fun!

However, the thought must have crossed her mind at some stage that she had better move back to the 'real world'. So she found herself in Melbourne, where she then promptly fell in love. Nevertheless, with adventure always close to her heart, it was time to head off again – this time with her love – and travel around Australia in a panel van. Career and children were not even on the radar. We (family and close friends) all thought driving a panel van around Australia would be interesting to say the least. But Lana had the time of her life exploring, relaxing and having a blast all the way around our beautiful country. The adventure finished, and a marriage proposal followed shortly after, which she accepted.

A new location and new career was to be her next adventure. Lana found her home in Albury, two hours from me, and a corporate career with an amazing global organisation that she has now been with for twelve years. My first niece entered the world eight years ago, then two years later my nephew arrived. I was stoked! Babies are my life, and these two were mine (well not really, but that's how it feels to me).

Lana and I are very different mothers, just as we are different humans. Lana is always calm and relaxed with the babies and I am very routine-focused and bustling with energy. But either way, it works, and together, it works like a dream. When we are together, our children receive the full benefits of our different approaches – I provide games, meals and busyness, while Lana provides the safe place for a cuddle, deep conversation and 100 per cent focus on what's important.

As we all know, though, life does not always go to plan. Over the last year, Lana has had her share of struggles and juggling priorities. People grow apart and values change, and this has led to her being a single working mum and facing life without a partner. But don't you worry about my sister – she is still a shining star, each day doing her best to make the world a better place. Lana's twelve-year career has just stepped up a notch with a promotion and together we have purchased a gorgeous little home for her and the kids.

Life is sometimes tough, but together we are strong.

So, you may ask, how did our relationship grow to be where it is today?

Lana and I both juggle work and kids but it is so different for each of us. My kids are bigger now, so this, combined with my choice of a flexible career, allows me to assist Lana with her little ones. There is nothing better for my soul than having two extras join my family for a week of the school holidays to help Lana manage full-time work.

We love to be inspired by each other. I love running, while Lana loves strength training. We are always keen to take on each other's passion, even if it hurts a lot. Only last weekend, Lana put on her big girl pants and travelled to do her first ever triathlon with me. I could not be any prouder of her doing it without complaint and just complete gratitude for the experience. We both also love travel, so when Lana earned an all-expenses-paid, first-class trip to the United States, I was more than happy to be her partner. Can you even imagine two sisters who are trying their best to keep food on their children's plates having the opportunity to fly first-class all over the US? We were not going to let any part of that experience be just okay. It was extraordinary!

And therein lies the key to our relationship. We are totally aware of our differences and we embrace them. We fully support each other. We love each other's children as if they were our own. We enjoy the ups and downs together. We laugh and cry at every possible opportunity. Most importantly, our love for each other is ever-growing and everlasting.

I always ask people which Disney character best represents them. I align with Tinkerbell. Years ago, when I asked Lana, she said she didn't know and would have to think about it. It was not until about six months later, with much thought and determination to have the right character, Lana excitedly told me that she knew who her Disney character was. 'I am Merriweather, Tinkerbell's sister, born of the same tear, as different as the seasons and sisters forever.'

A sister is both your mirror – and your opposite.

– Elizabeth Fishel

Our children learn the most from watching what we do, not what we tell them to do. So start being the example. If you are telling your children to follow their dreams, it's time for you to start showing them that you too are following yours.

20

Jen

Building a village and a business
on the other side of the world

Jen Murnaghan is an Irish ex-pat who, in 2014, created Digital Dandy, a business that offers creative digital marketing services to Tasmanian businesses. With nearly 20 years in marketing and creative production, beginning in Dublin, and moving to London, Sydney and now Hobart, Jen established her digital marketing agency to support local businesses who are looking to augment their voice online.

It was a warm summer afternoon in Dublin and the bay was shimmering in the sun. The Martello Tower sat solid on Sandycove Point, a familiar beacon to anyone going home. While I strolled along the seafront, lost in the picturesque view, I was interrupted by a fleeting vision – a daydream of sorts. It was an image of me, alone in a big city. I was walking, perhaps in a crowd, wearing a suit and a holding a brown case, a leather attaché with clasp and firm handle. And that was it, a split-second vision that stayed with me for years.

Born and bred in Ireland, I had dreams of becoming an architect, but my hopeless efforts in maths thwarted my success. I considered journalism for a while, but wasn't brave enough to take the leap, so I settled on a safe arts degree, studying English and Art History. I supported my ~~socialising~~ study with a job in my cousin's music store and proudly bought my first car – a white Golf – with the money I saved. The smell of independence was in the air.

With mainland Europe so close, travel was always aplenty. Our family spent summer holidays by the Mediterranean, with regular trips across the Irish Sea to satisfy our cultural curiosities. We drove across Dales to heritage homes, visited Churchill's birthplace – Blenheim Palace – and discovered the Yorkshire home of my favourite writing family, the Brontës. There were school exchanges to Germany and France, a stint as a sailing instructor in Manhattan, an adventure around Europe by train, an attempt to teach English in the north of France and a spontaneous trip to Budapest, where I found my first snowflake. I was struck by the magic of travelling, the experiences that could teach you so much. I had the bug and knew instinctively it was going to be hard to shake.

While life for a 22-year-old university graduate was filled with potential, and there were many moments of exhilaration, I suffered from a niggling yet exhausting lack of confidence. I had everything going for me, but the monkey on my back was pulling me down. That monkey was years later diagnosed as anxiety, a condition linked to my autoimmune disease. While I was often plagued by an awful sense of foreboding, I still had a strong desire for independence. I wanted to be something, on my own terms, and that vision, that brown case, kept coming back to haunt me. Much to the heartache of my family, I made a choice that year that would change my life forever. I left my parents and sisters, a long-term boyfriend, a burgeoning creative career, and moved to Australia for a supposed six-month sabbatical.

The bitumen at Bondi Beach could have cooked an egg. Like a true Irish tourist, I flicked off my runners and instantly burnt the soles of my feet. I didn't care. It was summer, I was with friends, and I was utterly anonymous. The following weeks had me working hard on a tan, eating juicy fruit salads, drinking late into the night, swimming, laughing and being utterly free. I was in heaven. This newfound sense of self had me completely enraptured and something deep inside clicked. It was a distinct physical experience, combined with another fleeting vision – this time, of not going home.

Looking back, working my way from barmaid to brand ambassador in Sydney took an incredible amount of grit. I had no real plan but I was sure I was in the right place. My sisters both came to Australia and had their own adventures. My parents also came for great visits, but for a while I had to detach myself from this core unit. While I'll admit to making lots of mistakes, I learnt more about myself than ever before. My anxiety stayed with me but my *joie de vivre* suppressed it for a time. I met my husband in March of my first year in Australia and our equally independent spirits magically combined, and a treasured friendship grew into love.

We married in 2003 and lived by the beach. Life was pretty good but took a new turn in 2007 with the end of my husband's business and the birth of our first child. With family in Ireland and New Zealand and a hazy future for both our careers, we knew we had some serious challenges ahead. Neither of us was interested in long commutes; nor did we entertain the idea of long hours at childcare. Rent for our tiny apartment was exorbitant, so it was time for a change. In October 2009, after an initial decision to move back to Ireland (the Irish economy had just collapsed the year we contemplated a move), we chose to stay in Australia and moved to Hobart, with two toddler boys in tow. We had visited a few times and I remembered how clear the air was. We had two local contacts but knew not a soul.

This was my second significant move within a decade, and while that may sound insignificant to some, it was a huge adjustment to a girl who suffered from a weak state of self-worth. Add in a whole lot of nappy brain and I was your typical basket case. We made it through the first few months – good work prospects were on the horizon for my husband, while I filled my days with playground adventures and sleepy drives deep into the countryside. There were very tough days when I would sit on the kitchen floor, numb to my surroundings, deeply cut with depressive thoughts, exhausted and desperately alone. What had we done? I was missing my independence, my sense of purpose, and needed an outlet to keep me afloat. I felt desperately alone.

Enter the Brothers Trimm and the start of my escape into mummy blogging. I created a blog that celebrated boyhood and had me connecting with people across the world. Every napping hour I spent at my computer, reading, writing and making friends with an online community filled with women like me. That experience – that escape from nappies and nightmares – was invigorating and fulfilling. A new calling, a new vision. I had found my new purpose.

Community has been defined as the condition of sharing certain attitudes and common interests. I like to think of Hobart as a melting pot for this type of shared living. In the early days, it was always a treat to find a free car space outside your favourite shop, share veggie-growing tips with neighbouring gardeners and exchange smiles with strangers on the street. These small yet significant observations were a far cry from our life in Sydney, where we never even spoke to the tenants next door! And what was even more apparent was the opportunity to create relationships around the head-spinning life of early childhood.

Moving to Hobart was always a risk, and we were often warned 'you'll have a hard time finding work down there.' The irony is that neither of us has ever been busier. While my husband's cooking career has blossomed at Mona (the Museum of Old and New Art), I quickly realised that I needed to create my own career. Working for an employer in a regular 9 to 5 job would be tricky for a family like us. With Vinnie's hours rather unfriendly and his salary our staple, I needed to be creative with my career choices.

So what did I do? I worked four jobs. I wrote for a kid's blog, I co-curated a market. I worked for a small family business, then as a children's bookseller, and I began a micro-business. All while the boys were preschoolers and all while blogging on the Brothers Trimm. Clearly this wasn't my seaside vision, so what was I trying to prove?

In 2013, I was diagnosed with Hashimoto's disease, an autoimmune disease that affects the thyroid. I was dragging my feet, forgetting my every move, overwhelmed by the laundry pile and overly sensitive all the time. I was pushing myself, kidding myself that multi-tasking was a sign of strength and that I never needed help and was totally okay. The diagnosis couldn't have come sooner and I remember feeling such a heavy weight lifted, knowing I wasn't actually going totally nuts. So there had to be more changes, new food choices, medication for the rest of my life and the start of some study into self-compassion. I slowly reduced my workload (it's still a work in progress), and have been blessed with dear friends who have stepped in when I was at my worst.

With this new vested interest in wellbeing, I worked hard on redefining my core values and finally began to recognise my potential. Life got easier as the boys began school and I realised it was okay to ask for help. Thanks to Vinnie and my Tassie friends, I got to discover a career that was right for me – a role where I could be independent, flexible and valued again.

Digital Dandy kind of happened by accident. When I had my tea towel design business, I was always online – blogging and posting on social media, sharing my story and developing the brand. It was my favourite part of the business. I hated the manufacturing side. **When I was asked to 'help out' with a friend's digital presence, I leapt at the chance and had my epiphany. All I needed was my laptop, some wifi and me – hooray! It made so much more sense – I could do school pick-up, be there for sports day, choose my hours and blend in with my peers.** Financially it actually looked viable and I was soon contributing the same income from this business as I did from all four of my part-time roles. With all the knowledge I had gained from experience, I decided to take the official leap.

Digital Dandy has been up and running for four years part-time, two years full-time, and I'm now looking to grow the team.

I get to collaborate, tell stories, share dreams and help plan them. I get the pressures of building a business – I'm slap bang in the middle of making it all work. I get to run workshops and coach businesses across the state. I share in the growing pains and swap stories with working parents. This is my happy place. While there are times of frustration (usually around the time when I want to do more but it's time for school pick-up), I envy how my husband can work all the hours he needs. There are the swimming and piano lessons, the nagging to manage. There's bedtime and weekend excursions to wrangle. There are days where I'll feel lonely and despondent, but thanks to life lessons I can now call for help without fear of failure. **I'm self-employed and self-sufficient. I'm working towards self-confidence with radical self-care. I'm independent while managing a privileged position as a mother and wife. I've learnt how to manage without family around me. I've learnt how to manage my mental health and self-doubt.**

I still have my leather case and it sits in my bedroom as a reminder of my past. It's now a container for my memories, my life chapters and goals. I'll keep it for the kids. Maybe we'll need two, in the hope they help them find their place and purpose, right here – or wherever their hearts lead them to.

Individually, we are one drop. Together, we are an ocean.
— Ryunosuke Satoro

When your kids are old enough, let them make their own lunches after dinner each night. We have a special 'lunch box' container with suitable items in our cupboard and fridge. The boys choose for themselves, which gives them a sense of empowerment while we know they are eating something decent each day. Our mornings? So much calmer.

21

JADE

Heart-centred entrepreneur travelling the world

Jade McKenzie is the founder of Event Head, a business specialising in helping entrepreneurs and business owners create purposeful and powerful events. She is also the editor of EH Magazine, *author of* The Ultimate Event Toolkit *and a professional speaker and workshop facilitator.*

This is for the mothers out there.

The mothers with bleary eyes, thin patience and constant overwhelm. With bins full of nappies, laundries full of dirty washing and sinks full of dishes.

This is for the mothers who know in their hearts that building their own business is the best way they can look after their family, but are overwhelmed at how it's going to happen. The mothers who know it's time to follow their dreams but at the same time, know that it's also time for maternal health nurse appointments, groceries and prescriptions for mastitis.

This is for the mothers who feel 'behind' as they watch others in their business communities kick ass, go from zero dollars to six figures and become an overnight success while they can't even find the time to shave their legs.

For you mothers, nodding your heads and silently screaming,

'Yes! That's me!' I want you to know.
You are not alone.
Everything will be okay.
How do I know? Because not long ago, I was you.

It only feels like yesterday that I found out I was pregnant. That tiny, precious baby I had longed for my whole life was suddenly a reality. Looking at those two pink lines on the pregnancy test gave me one surprisingly satisfying feeling.

Freedom.

Surprising, because I didn't realise this was what I was craving.
Satisfying, because I knew that this would change everything.
The birth of my baby was going to be the birth of the new me and a whole new adventure.

Subconsciously, I suppose I knew the universe was tugging me in a new direction. After three years managing and developing a small cancer charity into a national organisation with new and exciting member programs, a calendar full of fundraising events and community initiatives, national press and recognition and large corporate sponsors, it was fair to say that I was burnt out.

Hard work is in my blood, but the twelve-hour days, the stress of undertaking so many different roles, the constant contact with people my age who were sick and facing their mortality, and having to go to the funerals of those I had grown close to, began to taint everything with a heavy sadness. I couldn't separate myself from the organisation any more, and the never-ending dog paddle in a sea of overwhelm was leaving me weary.

I don't think I quite realised I felt all this until I had that pregnancy test in my hand. As the quote from *The Scarlet Letter* by Nathaniel Hawthorne goes: 'She had not known the weight until she felt the freedom.'

But what I did know, and have always known, was that I was being led on a different journey to those around me. My whole life I'd felt as if I was a square peg in a starburst hole and didn't understand why I wouldn't fit. I never wanted to settle. I always wanted to do big things. I never fitted the mould. I've always had a very strong and immense trust in the universe showing me the way. I just followed the clues until I found what felt like 'home'. For most of my life, these 'homes' had been temporary, but I knew that they would all eventually lead to that inner calling my soul had always told me was there. Like an onion, I had to peel the layers, do the work, cry the tears, until I reached what was inside.

Finally, it was time to step up and do the work I had been born to do. The funny thing is, though, I didn't know what that was. But despite this, I knew I'd be okay.

I knew that once my baby was born, so would a new chapter with all the answers I was ready for. And so, when I took that last step out of the office and organisation that I had put so much love into, to go on maternity leave, I knew I would never go back. And as sad as that was, it was the most liberating moment of my life.

I spent the next five weeks nesting, nurturing and impatiently waiting for my baby. When she finally arrived, I wondered what the hell I had got myself into! Ha!

It all feels like a blur now, but in the early days of motherhood – in between the constant changing of nappies, endless feeds and crazy highs and lows first-time parenting throws full force at you – a seed was planted. What if I gave people the gift of a moment, the gift of a memory to smile upon? What if I gave them the gift of connection?

Every single cell in my body tingled. Yes! That's the legacy I wanted to leave in this world. Connection, laughter, happiness, joy, love, presence.

Soon the dots connected and my beautiful business Event Head came to life. A business built around the things that I had brought to every job, friendship and relationship I cared for and adored. A business built around my own unique skills, strengths and loves. For the first time in my life, I was able to call all the shots and create something that was everything I ever wanted and needed in a career.

What an incredible opportunity I had been given! What an amazing thing to do for myself and my family. But I'm not going to lie to you, it was hard. What is it about motherhood that kicks every bit of self-doubt into overdrive? And guilt. Don't get me started on the guilt that pangs with every cry, every whimpering look and every thought around wanting to do something for yourself. I remember thinking, Someone please help, the hospital didn't flick on my selfless switch. I was still thinking about my own wants and needs and I was worried – was I a terrible mother?

The early months with my baby were filled with many delicious and awe-inspiring moments, but they were also punctuated with some real emotional and physical struggles. The cocktail of 'OMG, what the hell do we do? Is this normal? Google it!' mixed in with the hormonal crazies and a side of broken sleep gave me a hangover worse than what any amount of vodka could ever do.

Something that frequently penetrated my early thoughts was that I still wanted to do things, be things, achieve things and change things for the better. And for a little while there, that made me feel horrible. It was as if the one thing I had always wanted my whole entire life – a beautiful, healthy child – wasn't enough to sustain me, and I felt guilt in waves. I knew I wanted to have babies before I knew I wanted to get married! So why wasn't I like those mothers who wanted to stay home every day with their children and dedicate every minute to them? Why did I still have this immense desire to go out there and change the world in a way that I couldn't do in an office cubicle? Why couldn't I be happy to just be?

But it's not in me. My drive, my passions, my purpose only got bigger after Bun was born.

Now, more than ever, I had to be a role model. I had to show her how incredible this world can be when we believe in ourselves and step toward meaning and fulfilment in our lives.

The adventures we have been on are experiences I was never afforded as a child. The things I only came upon in my adult years are now being gifted to her as a young girl. And that makes me so happy. Four years on from when she was born, I can see clearly now that all of these things are my gift to her so she may grow into a strong, independent, kind and worldly young woman. I finally see that what I am doing is not selfish at all. Instead, it's pretty darn cool. She is constantly surrounded by a community of people who cherish her, adore her, and think she's one of the coolest kids they've ever met. She is learning about culture and how others live through our travels. She is seeing that there are different types of work and that one is not better than the other, it is just a choice. She knows that there is a big, wide world out there and that life is not confined to our four walls. This child has spirit and sass and the whole world at her feet.

It has felt like a long road to get here. In this short amount of time, it has felt as if one hundred years could have passed since giving birth. But my gosh, what incredible lessons have been learnt along the way. What a lesson in personal development – having a baby and starting a business! That was no learning curve; it was a learning mountain.

Even now when the physical pain has disappeared, sleep is again our friend and we see this amazing being grow and develop in so many incredible ways, there are still pangs of guilt, even when you know you are making the right decision for your child, your family and yourself. Babies and business. Never have two things seemed so polar opposite and yet so intertwined. You certainly don't stop being a mother when you work on your business and you certainly don't stop being a business owner when you are in mum mode. At times, it can feel like a real boxing match trying to get these two responsibilities to align.

Luckily for me, the universe showed me the light and today I am surrounded by strong, incredible women who show me what is possible and reinforce the fact that I am a good mum, doing good things. And I hope that by sharing my story with women, being as open and transparent as possible in my everyday life and by supporting mothers who come into my community, I can show them what is possible – and perhaps even inspire them to be kinder and more loving towards themselves. We are not terrible people for having needs. We are not bad mums for feeling conflicted or sad or stressed. We are simply human, and we forget that that's okay.

Sometimes, you don't lose yourself when you have a baby. Sometimes, you finally find yourself. And in finding yourself, you show your own children, and other mothers, just what we are all capable of.

It is okay to want to build a beautiful business while your babe is young.

It is okay to have your own ambitions and dreams.

It is okay to want more so you can build an ideal life for you and your family.

You *can* do both well and still be kind to yourself.

You *can* navigate the challenges and bumps in the road in an empowered way.

You *can* inspire your children through your actions.

You *can* be a happy mum and a kick-ass business woman without feeling you're doing a half-assed job.

You *can* involve your children in your business without feeling unprofessional.

You *can* use your children as your inspiration to help your businesses grow.

You *can* have a soulful and deep connection with your children no matter how many hours you work.

Some days I still feel so overwhelmed that only chocolate, a sad movie and some tears will fix it, but I know that there are other mums out there who understand and have my back, as I have theirs.

It's your time to shine, mama.

Stay on the same page with a printed family calendar placed in the kitchen. Use this to record all your individual commitments in advance and identify when you need extra assistance with the kids or times you need to juggle work. And don't forget to pull it out when your husband says you didn't tell him about an upcoming event!

22

Louise

Freelance writing and editing

Louise Correcha is the founder of Hummingbird Writing, a business that helps organisations and professionals boost the readability and written standard of their reports, manuals, proposals, technical papers and books. She previously taught English to adults. Louise adores listening to, breaking down, analysing and learning new languages and alphabets. She has co-authored and lent her voice to various resources to help people learn both English and Spanish.

In a speech for Oprah's *SuperSoul Sunday* series, the writer Elizabeth Gilbert talks about how passion manifests itself for two very different kinds of people in this world – the jackhammers and the hummingbirds. Her explanation ends up validating pretty much my whole life, including the decisions I have made as a working mum.

Not bad for one speech.

The jackhammers, she explains, are the Elizabeths of the world. Those who've always known their passion and have woken each day to stubbornly and diligently work in pursuit of it.

Then there are the hummingbirds, who do things quite differently. They fly around the gardens of the world, sampling the different flowers. I like to imagine this might mean bookkeeping one day, screenwriting the next. Or real estate followed by jewellery design. Or one day, after doing all *that*, they realise that inventing uniquely delicious ice cream flavours is actually the thing that they absolutely, positively must be doing. Basically, hummingbirds humbly follow the crumbs of curiosity the universe has generously sprinkled along their life paths.

Pretty cool, right? And not just because it means the next time someone implies I might be procrastinating, I can tell them that I'm actually a hummingbird following the crumbs of curiosity on my life path. But I digress

We clearly owe a great debt to the jackhammers of the world – those whose tenacity and single-mindedness has led to amazing works of art and literature, feats of engineering, and some of the greatest discoveries of humankind. But the service of the hummingbirds is just as important. Flitting between fields and realities, hummingbirds cross-pollinate the world with ideas and perspectives, keeping human culture open and oxygenated. Breathing.

The problem is, a whole culture has been built around the belief that once we find our passion, we will feel fulfilled. This follow-your-passion movement, while so benevolent in intention, has unfortunately been making a lot of lovely little hummingbirds feel increasingly anxious. That there's something wrong with them because they're 30, or 40, or 60, and still don't know what they want to be when they grow up. I can relate.

You see, I have never completely belonged in one place, or with one particular group of people. I'm scholarships and

straight A+s and Bach, but also Barnesy and wagging school and smoking with the cool kids. I appreciate the gravitas of Kubrick's musical choices for *2001: A Space Odyssey*, but am just as enraptured with ACDC's 'Thunderstruck'.

I've also had lots of different jobs. These have included petrol station attendant and CEO-speech editor. Lemon-box packer and grapevine pruner. Adult literacy program coordinator. Administrator. Flower bulb-planter. Business-writing trainer. Electricity-bill-error corrector. Company director. English teacher to people from around the world. And a damn fine fish 'n' chip-shop worker.

Each job taught me valuable life skills and knowledge – not the least of which, of course, was how to count to five in Greek, thanks to the fish 'n' chip shop. It was there that I also made my first foray into interpreting other alphabets, as I pored over *Neos Kosmos* while folding boxes and waiting for dim sims to fry.

I also remember a woman coming into the petrol station one day with her daughter, and asking if there was a man who could help her choose the right oil for her car. I wanted to tell her exactly what I thought about her teaching her daughter *that* little gem of a lesson. And how if anyone at that place knew anything about cars, it was most certainly me, with a mechanic for a dad who'd made sure I knew a hell of a lot more than just what type of oil to use in my car before I was allowed to drive it alone. Instead, I smiled, asked about her car, and helped her choose the right oil. I like to hope her daughter learnt something that day, and not just about oil. It also, of course, confirmed what I would certainly *not* say or do if I ever had a daughter.

One of the most important crumbs of curiosity that I followed early in my life was the one my dad brought home for me when I was fourteen. It was a brochure about scholarships to undertake a student exchange program. I followed it, and at sixteen I was living with a beautiful Czech host family and attending Czech high school for a year. This led to university studies in linguistics, Russian, anthropology and English teaching, and more immersion in other languages and cultures in the years that followed. This in turn helped me develop the skills and experience to start my first business in communications training and coaching in my late twenties.

Despite all the flitting around in life, though, writing was always there – even if it was like a jackhammer fading in and out of volume, jutt-jutting away in a distant street. But I struggled a bit with the idea that I wasn't what the dominant cultural narrative had taught me a writer was *supposed* to be. Sure, I wrote stories for my younger cousins as a child and won spelling competitions. (I remember repeatedly spelling *miscellaneous* in my head.) I was *happy* when a relative gave me a *Roget's Thesaurus* for my ninth birthday. I also went on to be awarded some significant scholarships, mainly off the back of my writing skills. But I didn't *need* to constantly write. I most certainly could not be bothered keeping a journal, despite being told repeatedly that that is what writers absolutely, positively must do. I still can't.

I didn't really connect with most of my classmates or teachers in university literature and writing classes. Also, I sucked at being pained and tortured. Give me a difficult situation in life and I'll probably put a positive spin on it. Again, not what *serious* writers did, right? (It would be years before I would hear the author

Gary Shteyngart talk about the tendency in some of the world's best-known storytelling traditions – Irish and Russian in particular – to 'take all of the tragedy and whack it over the head with humour, over and over again'.)

Again and again, I left writing to the side. Usually because I was too busy working in a 'real' job.

In 2008, my husband and I started our company – offering language and communications coaching and training – after an extended backpacking honeymoon in which we'd decided to start a business. We threw ourselves into the business and, with sacrifice, slowly built it. The only problem was that the unique skills and knowledge that enabled us to best serve our clients meant it was hard to find anyone to help us do that work, so that we could occasionally step back and work 'on' rather than 'in' the business.

As great as the experience was, we realised the business model was unsustainable. I was burnt out. We needed to step out and reassess the business direction. So in 2011 we took an extended break in my husband's home country of Colombia. We sold everything we owned to pay for the break. We worked on our business ideas in the local library, but also spent time relaxing with family, eating home-cooked meals and home-grown mangoes, and dozing in hammocks. And, of course, I embraced the very important work of sending text messages to save my favourites in that year's crop of Colombian *X-Factor* hopefuls.

After a few months, the time came to return home. Bills were mounting and savings were draining. I knew I wasn't yet ready to jump back into the stresses of either teaching or self-employment. But what would I do?

One day, while searching jobs online, the thought popped into my head to enter the keyword 'proofreader'. And there appeared an advertisement for the job I would hold for the next four years – years that would include the birth of our child.

I met with the awesome recruiter who would go on to recommend me for the role. I remember him being worried that I might be bored in the job, which involved sitting by myself tweaking language in highly technical documents. But after years of teaching and running a business, I could think of nothing more appealing than being left alone to methodically and meditatively work. To sit with sentences. To quietly delight in the difference I could make by moving a comma, inserting a dash or changing a word. The recruiter and I ended up giggling at the slightly disturbing enthusiasm with which I expressed my love for punctuation in particular. He was equal parts happy and worried, which is always an excellent combination I think.

As well as loving being left alone to do my job, I also loved working with other people again. Chats in the lunchroom. Laughter around the coffee machine. Friday night drinks with a really cool bunch of colleagues. The workplace culture was excellent – fun but highly professional and respectful. I was part of one of the most competent and efficient administration teams I've ever come across, and I continue to be grateful for the many tricks I learnt working with them. The company also followed an exceptional style guide for writing, written by one of the founders of the business. I relished being able to correspond with the author of the guide over the intricacies of style and grammar in writing, and being able to learn from and work to such high standards.

Most of all, I loved finishing work at 5 o'clock, walking out the door and – without a smidgeon of guilt – not giving it another second's thought until the next day.

Five months after I started the job, we discovered I was pregnant. I had to tell my manager straight away, because I had found out the day before a champagne breakfast event, and she was wondering why I was drinking juice! She was super supportive, though, and I ended up working until the 38th week of pregnancy.

In July 2013, our daughter was born, arriving into the world with bright eyes and a bright smile (really). We were living in a beachside western suburb of Melbourne, where everything we needed was within walking distance. So, despite the extreme sleep deprivation we were hit with as parents to a baby who seemingly hadn't got the memo that newborns were supposed to be 'sleepy', we could at least walk along the beach, sit down at a café and feel like we were still human beings. Even if we more closely resembled those of the night-of-the-living-dead variety.

When my daughter was around six months old, work asked if and how I'd like to return. I am so grateful I had such an excellent employer, especially considering how many others have to deal with employers with such short-term views on their staff spending a small portion of their lives doing what is arguably the most important job for the future of humanity. (But hey, let's not let *that* get in the way of next year's sales targets, right?) So I started to work from home a couple of days a week. Over the next year, I gradually built up the time I worked and transitioned from working from home to working at the office as my daughter grew and could last longer between breastfeeds. My husband and I somehow managed the juggle, initially with the help of a stint at childcare (when we moved back to the city for a bit), and then two phenomenal family daycare educators once we moved back to the western suburbs.

My role by then had evolved past the original job description. I continued to enjoy work and the opportunities it gave me. I also took on committee roles and writing and public-speaking engagements, and started independently taking courses to further build my skills as a technical writer – a career option I still might pursue at some stage. After one of these courses, I was engaged by the principal of the technical writing consultancy that ran the course, to provide editorial assistance on his latest book. It's an area I continued to keep in the back of my mind.

Eventually, though, after almost four years in the job I felt the urge to move on to the next challenge. But I wouldn't be me if I didn't then go and enthusiastically make a nice big mistake in the pursuit of life experience. So, with immense gratitude to my employer, I resigned, and in a moment of slight madness, took another job I was offered.

I kind of knew that that job was a mistake – not because of the work itself, but rather the full-time hours and the workplace culture (aspects of which were made pretty clear in the interview). But I convinced myself that it would be fine. Plus, I've always believed that it's better to regret something you did than something you didn't. So I went for it.

I didn't even last three weeks. For someone usually extreme in her stoicism and loyalty, this was new.

In those three weeks, I suffered a constant internal battle. On the one side, the 'there's a reason for everything' me was asking,

Is this a challenge the universe is presenting? An opportunity to learn a skill that will come in handy in future?

On the other side, another part cautioned, *Maybe, but these problems actually should not be yours to fix* and *If you're feeling like this already, it's actually better that you leave now rather than when you're already involved with important projects and clients.*

And, finally, *Look, if you are going to be away from that little girl who you miss so excruciatingly that you sometimes feel an invisible cord physically pulling you back to her, it had better bloody be worth it!*

Street-smart Louise dropped a truth bomb on me as only a true friend can. And this time, I listened to her, rather than my usual trick of politely smiling and nodding then turning around and carrying on regardless, as if in some sort of battle to prove my worth to the world.

Well, not any more. My world had now made abundantly clear just how much worth she thought I had. In her smile and her strong, tiny arms thrown around my neck.

I was determined to create a working situation in which I could do what I knew I could do well while prioritising my daughter.

I wanted to be there as much as possible for her. For her made-up songs. For her wise life observations – the type only young children can make. And late at night, when she should probably be asleep but she's engineered her own roller skates from Duplo train carriages and wants me to join her as Elsa 'ice skating' (yes, she's quite sure they're ice skates and not roller skates), **I wanted to live that moment without anxiety about being presentable for work the next day. Because I happen to believe that those moments are our chance to get about as close to the magic of life as we're ever going to.**

I decided to focus on growing the business back up, but this time around the editing and writing I'd always dabbled in but never focused on.

Writing and editing from home now means I can drop my daughter off to family daycare and be home working five minutes later. Even though I sometimes miss working with others, and I have to be careful not to get distracted by other things at home, I don't need to waste time and money getting ready for and travelling to work. I can maximise the time I have outside of caring for my daughter. It suits me in this season of life.

It also suits my personality to work across different sectors. I do everything from suggesting improved content for a government communications campaign to editing annual reports, books or technical conference papers. I also write things like feature articles, newsletters for small businesses and award nominations for prominent business and public-service professionals. The best part is that in doing so, I continue to learn lots of different things about lots of different fields. Right up my hummingbird alley. Plus, it's rewarding when my clients tell me that what I wrote was just what they had wanted to say but couldn't quite find the words for.

Of course, it's not always easy. The work is unpredictable and sometimes involves late nights and early mornings turning a job around quickly. I might be in the supermarket answering an urgent email or text from a client asking me to approve a final proof or help rephrase an important sentence. I'm often juggling several urgent pieces. But I wouldn't change it for anything.

One morning late last year, I did a little experiment. After 36 years, I decided to declare something to the universe. I updated my usually lengthy, descriptive LinkedIn title with one word: *Writer*.

At 2 pm that day, I was in an office being interviewed for a job as a freelance copywriter for an awesome Melbourne design agency (effectively making them one of the regular clients of my business). This was a job I hadn't applied for. It was as if the universe had just been waiting for me to make up my mind already. Smiling and nodding encouragingly, but also rolling her eyes just a little bit.

As Elizabeth Gilbert goes on to say as she wraps up that speech:

If you're willing to just release yourself from the pressure and anxiety surrounding passion, and you just humbly and faithfully continue to follow and trust the hummingbird path … one of these days you might just look up and realise, 'Oh my word, I am exactly where I'm meant to be. I'm with the people I'm supposed to be with; I'm doing the work I'm supposed to be doing … In other words, if you can just let go of passion, and follow your curiosity, your curiosity just might lead you to your passion.

In the end, I think parenthood strips you to your core in a way that gives you no choice but to rebuild yourself around that core. That might just be one of its greatest gifts.

So yes, being a hummingbird has led to some pretty interesting things in my life. But thanks to motherhood, that jackhammer that was also always there – although fading in and out – has now grabbed its chance to be unapologetically loud. To no longer be ignored.

Now, about those ice-cream flavours …

We recently discovered a meal subscription service at a local café. It's actually a registered charity, and you get excellent quality, nutritious chef-made meals at a super low cost. We get the minimum five meals weekly – because we still like to cook – but just having those five meals ready means we're covered for two or three nights mid-week (or for my lunches, seeing as I work from home). This reduces work around cooking and cleaning up for a couple of days, plus it's cheaper and healthier than takeaway. It's a great balance for us.

23

Carly and Alee

IVF, family and finances

Carly Naughton is a stay-at-home mum and author of the popular blog Perils of a Passable Parent. Alee Fogarty is a tattoo artist and graphic designer. Carly and Alee rose to fame when the birth of their son, who was conceived by IVF, was featured on Australian television, and when a subsequent Facebook post by Alee about their family went viral. Carly and Alee have since become the first Australian same-sex couple to be married under the new legally binding Evermore Pledge.

I always wanted to be a million different things growing up. From a palaeontologist to an archaeologist to a veterinarian. One thing that never changed, however, was that I wanted to be a mother. Finding out in my early twenties that I had endometriosis, and that I would require IVF if I ever wanted a family, was a crushing blow.

Skip forward a few years and I met Alee. She was a tattooist and had tattooed one of my friends, so I added her on Facebook to check out more of her work. I was honest with her from very early on about my infertility.

I had always been working or studying. My parents both had a very strong work ethic as I was growing up, and this was passed on to all my siblings and me. After school, I completed a degree in anthropology, as well as a few other diplomas and qualifications along the way. When I met Alee, I was working at a tattoo studio and studying. Once we began dating, I managed to land a dream job that held very exciting career growth prospects for the future.

That job was working in a foster care agency, supporting the foster carers and also ensuring that the children were being placed into suitable homes. It was not an easy job. Daily I would read endless referrals for children coming into care or being moved from placement to placement, with each referral outlining just some of the abuse that the children had lived with. It was also a highly stressful job, with deadline after deadline, legal forms that needed lodging on time, case notes that had to be uploaded and countless meetings, emails and phone calls.

It was the kind of job where you are stuck in the middle of a situation but you can only do so much, because the Department of Child Safety would have the final say in all decisions. Sometimes I would question those decisions. Not that I would get anywhere. I would then have my carers calling, asking why something had not been done or why a certain decision had been made, but it was beyond my pay grade. That was not a decision I had any kind of power over. There were many nights I would spend the drive home crying over something that had happened that day. I would question myself over and over as to whether I could have done more to find a home for the ten-plus kids that came into care right on 5 pm. Should I have pushed our carers harder to take more kids than they had room for? It was very hard and very stressful.

We began our first cycle of IVF in early 2013. We were amazed when I fell pregnant the first time. Unfortunately, I lost this baby early in the pregnancy. We then did another cycle once money allowed, however we lost another baby in the first trimester. Finally, after two fresh cycles, one frozen and two miscarriages, we were successful with our third fresh cycle. I gave birth to our son in August 2015.

I initially took maternity leave for twelve months, then extended it for another six. The week before I was due to start back I wrote a budget including daycare two days per week, factoring in Alee needing to take a day off to look after our son (often she will work at least one of her days off each week), two hours driving daily, four tolls per day, my emotional health working in such a high-stress job, and then only seeing my son when he first wakes and right before going to bed on the days I work, and weighed that against what my résumé was going to look like if there was a giant gap where I was an unpaid stay-at-home mother.

Looking down at the budget I had written, I realised that financially we were no better off at all if I returned to work. It worked out about even, maybe even slightly worse because of the fact that Alee would no longer be able to pick up a day's work if we needed the extra cash.

I posted in my trusty mother's group asking advice because it really worried me having a huge gap of unemployment on my résumé. One mother wrote, 'If you are considering being broke and barely seeing your child just so your résumé looks good, you really need to rethink that.' She was right. Almost every mum that commented was in the same boat. They could not return to work because they could not afford it. Daycare fees are just ridiculous.

I immediately phoned my boss and emailed him my resignation. Being a father and grandfather himself, he was incredibly understanding. He told me I should consider studying part-time while not working so I could keep my skills relevant and current for when I was ready to return to work, which I decided I would definitely do. As soon as I got off the phone it felt as if a giant weight I didn't know existed had lifted off me. I had no idea the stress I was already under just at the thought of returning to work.

Once I fell pregnant, we'd agreed to be part of the TV show *Gold Coast Medical*. Alee's idea, not mine. The end of my pregnancy, our story and our son's birth were all aired on nationwide (and now international) TV. The episode was only minutes in when our phones blew up with messages and friend requests. Lesbians can be like that! Fast-forward a few months, and a post Alee made on Facebook – which was our family photo with a little story about how a woman had approached us asking whose baby our son was, and how she didn't seem to comprehend that we were a couple and he was the baby of both of us – went insanely viral. No idea how the hell this happened. She posted it, we went to dinner and by the time we finished, Alee's phone had died from all the notifications. The photo was everywhere, and I mean *everywhere*. Someone told us that a UK sperm bank was using it for their promo stuff, which was weird. It was liked and shared hundreds of thousands of times in a matter of days. Once again, our inboxes were flooded.

So many same sex, trans and intersex couples were asking us for advice on how to start a family. People were sharing their coming-out stories with us and even some parents were saying our story made them realise that their children being gay was not the end of the world. Many people saw us as just a family, because that is what we are. Then again, there were also hundreds, maybe thousands, of negative and disgusting comments. How can two women raise a boy to be a man? Why did we adopt a black baby? (Our son is African American.) We were race traitors, we would hang, devil's spawn and so on. We felt sad, but not for us. We felt sad for those people who hold such hatred within themselves and put so much energy into their negativity. But we embraced the positivity and love, and the response is still overwhelming.

Blogger Constance Hall shared the post and suddenly we were being approached for all kinds of things. I have been asked to blog for numerous websites. Monash IVF and the company SuperCare are helping us to access our superannuation so we can begin another IVF cycle. We've even written this chapter for this book! I now count managing our bookings and writing my own blog and social media as my occupation.

I feel incredibly lucky that Alee is in the kind of job where she can always work more if we need more money, and also that we live in a country where we are fortunate enough to receive money to assist us to raise our family. Many mothers have said to me that they wished they could stay home with their children until the children begin school, but it wasn't an option for them. I also know others who returned to work as soon as they could, because being home 24/7 with limited adult contact drove them absolutely insane. I have friends who work and their kids are in daycare and they bring in maybe an extra $100 a week, but that is the sacrifice they make for their children because that $100 is make-or-break for them.

I don't think there is a right or wrong when it comes to working and raising children. Each family and financial situation is different and as long as the parents are doing what is best for them and their children, it can't be wrong. My résumé may look a bit shit down the track, but hey, I am doing a job I love every single day (for free). It is hard work but it is damn rewarding. Who else can say they love their job and that they go to bed looking forward to seeing their boss in the morning?

Alee has always been artistic. Her mother once told me that she owes it to her because she gave Alee crayons and colouring pencils as soon as she could hold them. She has been tattooing now for over ten years. Being lesbian (I use this word loosely as neither of us really likes to define ourselves this way, labels are for jars, not people), Alee obviously has a lot of LGBTQIA clients, and word spreads quickly throughout the community, so her client base continues to grow rapidly.

Because of her work, Alee was already quite well known in 'the scene' when we met. You drop her name to a group of lesbians and I guarantee at least one of them will know her, or know of her. But then again, the gay scene is extremely small in that sense. Everyone knows everyone through dating, friends or drama.

After years of working for free or very, very bare minimum wage while she was doing her apprenticeship, she has now put in the hard yards and can earn herself decent coin, thankfully.

Alee was working in a small, run-down shop on the Gold Coast when we first met. She had been there for years and was really unhappy. She had it out with her boss after a lot of built-up crap and now is working at the very same shop that I was working at when we first met. She is so happy there and thinks of her boss like extended family. They treat her well and give her freedom to work as much or as little as she wants, which in turn makes her happy and encourages her to want to work and earn more. It is the kind of job that gives her unlimited flexibility, really, and her clients are also like extended family, with many being loyal to her throughout her career. Because of this, they are understanding when she needs to cancel work at the last minute if I get sick, or if our son has something on that she needs to attend.

I always wanted to be a million different things growing up. One thing that never changed, and still hasn't, was wanting to be a mother. It is the most rewarding job I've ever done, with one of the coolest bosses I've ever met.

> Everyone assumes they know what's best for your children. Ask yourself, 'Am I doing the best I can?' and if you can answer yes, then you are doing it right! F**k what anyone else says about how you should parent your child.

24

JESSICA

Reskilling and re-entering the workforce

Jessica Sjöhage is a Swedish mum of three and a certified personal trainer living on the small farm she and her Australian husband own just outside Melbourne. Jessica shares snippets of her life, complete with recipes and updates on her sheep, horses and veggie garden, on Instagram.

As a young girl, I was absolutely fascinated by Australia. I used to read novels about life in the bush. I imagined the sunburnt country and living on a farm with horses. When I was eighteen years old, I applied for a job as a nanny with a Swedish family living on a farm in Noosa, Queensland, but I didn't get the job. So, I started saving up some money and when I was twenty years old, I had saved enough money to travel to the land of my dreams. I left Sweden and backpacked around Australia for five months. Little did I know that a couple of years later I would meet Michael and fall in love in the little Austrian ski resort of St Anton – of course, he was from Australia.

As a young woman with big dreams and a zest for life, it was really exciting to have an Aussie boyfriend. Australian men were so different from what I had experienced before, and I didn't think about the future or what it would actually mean if we had children together. We travelled around the world for a few years before we decided to settle down in Australia. I applied to RMIT University in Melbourne and finished a Bachelor of Arts in public relations three years later.

While I was studying hard, I still managed to have three jobs on the side. I have always loved working and meeting new people. I worked at Kathmandu (which allowed me to invest in some awesome travel gear), at the Crown Casino as a hostess (which satisfied my need for some glamour), and at a pub in Port Melbourne.

After university I got a full-time job in public relations, but after a year Michael and I thought it would be a good idea to give life in Sweden a go before we settled down properly. We needed to figure out where we actually wanted to settle. I got my permanent residency just before we left, so we knew that we had about a three-year period in which we could travel, or stay in Sweden, before returning to Australia (due to the immigration regulations back then).

In Sweden, we both got jobs and really enjoyed the lifestyle, the ready access to nature and the proximity to the rest of Europe. We would go to Ireland one weekend, Croatia the next. While in Sweden, I fell pregnant with twins and we were over the moon! I kept working at a Swedish newspaper in the advertising and sales department for as long as I could, but it was a difficult pregnancy, and after 25 weeks I could not work any more because much of my work included walking and seeing clients. That was the last time I worked in paid employment. This was eleven years ago.

The twins were born prematurely and they were tiny. To be honest, I can't remember much of that first year as we were living through the same chaos as most first-time parents. Sleep deprivation and just trying to stay sane. Never would I have thought that parenthood was going to be so hard.

We had settled very nicely into the Swedish lifestyle but we knew that we had a limited time before we would have to move back to Australia. When the twins were nine months old, I had to say goodbye to all family and friends – my entire support network. I was heartbroken and so were my parents.

I always intended to go back to work after a year or so, which I would have done had we stayed in Sweden, but when we moved back to Melbourne I didn't have a job to return to, and I never realised how expensive childcare was for two little people.

I was very happy to be a stay-at-home mum. I used to go to 'Swedish playgroup', I was on a number of committees and I never got bored with being at home. When the girls were three years old, I gave birth to my third child, another beautiful daughter. This made it even harder to go back to work. I know that I was fortunate to be able to stay at home with the children and that many people can't afford to do this, but we decided to make sacrifices and to live on Michael's wage. It wasn't easy and there were many times that I thought about getting back into the workforce as I felt guilty not working. But in truth, I had completely lost my confidence and didn't know what I would be able to do and how it would fit in with the children.

I used to be quite confident, but something happened while I was a stay-at-home mum. I lost track of who I was. I was so busy being a mum, doing what 'great mums' do, whatever that is. For me it was baking, cooking, taking the children to the zoo, the science museum, the aquarium and the various playgrounds in our area, and this was more than a full-time job. I never got bored, but I could feel I had lost my confidence somewhere along the way and I started thinking, *I don't know anything any more, I can't go back into PR, who would actually employ me? I don't want to work full-time, so what can I do?*

Somewhere deep inside I understood that I was employable, just perhaps not in the public relations industry any more because I had been out of it for such a long time. I never really loved it anyway. I was, however, thinking about working in sales, event planning or anywhere that I could work with people. I have great people skills and I am highly organised. And although I knew this, I still doubted myself.

Perhaps it was just procrastination, but I decided to wait until my youngest started school. I wanted to give her the same support I had given the twins. This meant that by the time I could start looking for work, I would have been a stay-at-home mum for over ten years!

One thing that kept me sane during those early years, and still today, was my gym time. That was my 'me time'. This didn't happen suddenly, though – I have always been very active. At the gym, I found inspiration to work hard and to stay active. I met some amazing women – some of them much older than me – who inspired me to keep fit. They made me realise how important it is to stay healthy, not just for your own sake but also for your children's. I wanted to be able to keep up with them at the playground, and when we were going for bike rides and swims. I realised that health is wealth.

Somewhere along the way, I started thinking about how fun it would be to be surrounded by positive, like-minded people. I thought, *If they can do it, so can I.* It still took me quite some time to find the courage to start the new path toward becoming a personal trainer. *I'm no Michelle Bridges*, I thought, *I'm not skinny and I do love wine and cheese, could I actually help someone and possibly inspire people?*

I used to chat at drop-off times to another school mum, Danielle. She told me about an expo that she had just organised that was designed for mothers who wanted to work, but couldn't find flexible career opportunities. Unfortunately, I couldn't attend on the day, but she gave me a goodie bag of information that contained fitness magazines from Fernwood Fitness (a women's gym). I had never been to a Fernwood gym before, but I loved the content of their magazines. I was given a contact at their head office and before I knew it, I had signed up to do Certificate III and IV in Fitness and Personal Training! I felt a bit embarrassed telling people about my plans. I thought they might judge me or laugh at me, but everyone was excited. I'm really grateful for that conversation that day at school drop-off! People often seem to enter your life at the right time.

During the course of my studies, we also decided to make a tree change. We had been living by the sea for many years and although we loved the location and the closeness to the city, we had both dreamt of having horses and other animals and to live a more balanced and healthy lifestyle. We found a beautiful property northeast of Melbourne.

The year 2016 was very busy for us. While I was organising the move and all it entailed, finding a new school for the children and researching the new area, I also had to study. I found the course a lot harder than I thought it would be and I struggled a bit. I had always been the mum who helped out in the classroom and on sport days, and I used to go to the gym four or five times a week, but suddenly I didn't have time for anything else apart from studying. No-one else put any pressure on me but myself, but it was a difficult adjustment going from being a stay-at-home mum in a small house with a small backyard, to being a student with three children and a farm to look after. Within a few months of living on the farm, we had eleven sheep, three horses, two turtles, six chooks, one dog and a huge garden to look after. I was suddenly living on a farm, with horses, in Australia – the life I imagined as a young girl.

The hardest part of the move was that we didn't have any support network near our new home. I had become used to not having my family around, but we used to live near Michael's parents and sister. Suddenly, I couldn't call them if I needed help with school pick-up or if the children were sick, or if I had an appointment. I didn't really know anyone either who would be able to help out. It is never easy to move away from friends and family, but we fell in love with the farm and felt that although it was a hard decision, it was the right one.

After a year of studying hard, I finished my course in December 2016 and took a well-deserved break over the children's school holidays. It was so lovely to spend time with them and just hang out and not be stressed about my studies.

So, what will the future hold? As part of the course, I had to write a business plan. With that in mind, I started planning and thinking about the future and what I could do once I had the certificates. An idea popped into my head to set up a 'women's boot camp' business at home. We have 15 acres, an arena, and lots of hills that you can run up and down. There is plenty of room for a group of people to exercise. I would be happy for women to bring their children along if this makes it easier for them to get out and stay active and strong while they are at home with little children. Not only will this enable them to exercise, they will also build camaraderie and friendships in the community. I am also slowly building up my home gym, so that I can have one-on-one personal training sessions.

I have set up an Instagram account called 'swaussiemum' because I thought it would be interesting for people to see who I am and what I do, especially when I start advertising my business. I want people to feel comfortable with me, who I am and what I stand for. My goal is to be an advocate for 'everything in moderation' and try to inspire people to find a great balance in life. We beat ourselves up if we don't lose weight or we feel guilty if we have some chocolate or a glass of wine mid-week. To me, it's more about being happy, strong, healthy and fit, not necessarily skinny. I want to be there for my children and be the mum who plays with them at the playground. Again, health is wealth.

I am now really excited about the future and what it holds. I understand that I am at the beginning of this new journey and I will have to work hard to make a name for myself. It seems like the 'perfect job in the industry' is difficult to find if you still want to be a stay-at-home mum, therefore I will focus on setting up my own business.

I hope I can be a role model for other women, and with my background, I am hoping that they will be able to relate to me because I understand the day-to-day struggles and pressures many of us feel in life.

> As a mum of three primary school-age girls, I always make sure that I prepare most of their school lunches the night before. All I have to make in the morning is their sandwiches. This frees up time to plait their long hair. I also set my drip coffee machine on a timer so I can enjoy my coffee first thing in the morning before waking up the kids.

25

Amanda

Personal boundaries as a working mum

Amanda Abel is a mum, paediatric psychologist and business owner. She founded Northern Centre for Child Development in Melbourne to offer paediatric clinical excellence to the community while providing a family-friendly working environment for herself and her team.

Growing up in Melbourne as the daughter of two South African immigrants, I adopted what I now see as some inherently South African traits. And I'm not talking about the few random words I used to say as a child in a South African accent without realising that was not how they were said by Aussies! I'm talking about thinking big and innovation. South Africa tends to be a culture of creative people who think outside the square. I'm pretty sure they developed their own motor fuel last century, which would have come in super handy during sanctions when trade restrictions were very much in place.

So I'm a natural improver, innovator and creator. When I was about seventeen, I thought of an awesome idea for a website where people listed their used cars and users could search the make and model of car they wanted to buy. Years later, Australia's most well-known car-selling website was launched and I was gutted I hadn't had the nous to actually act on my clearly good idea! I know my passion for innovation and change must have been incredibly annoying for many previous employers, when I would march into their offices and declare my ideas and outline why things in the workplace should change, why we should get a coffee machine, repaint, relocate ... But it has been a strength that's come in pretty handy while working for myself and, when paired with a bit of restraint at the right times, may have contributed to the success I've experienced.

Let me start by saying, I don't feel #blessed #thankful or #honoured to be where I am. I work bloody hard to (try to) be successful as a parent, wife, psychologist, manager and business owner and it has very little to do with luck. Careful decisions have been deliberated over during the three years I've been running my practice. These decisions and the time dedicated to them have come at sacrifices in other areas of my life. A tightrope has been constantly teetered upon! There have been monumental F-ups, tears and disappointments. The metaphorical towel has almost been thrown in at least twice. But it hasn't been all bad. I promise.

After initially studying music at university, I trained as a psychologist and was on the verge of a career change (which I now acknowledge was triggered by burn-out) when I fell pregnant shortly after getting married. Becoming a mum to my beautiful daughter has been the most rewarding experience of my life. Thankfully it renewed my passion for psychology and I returned to work by starting up my own private practice. My business is a multidisciplinary paediatric practice in Melbourne's north. I'm privileged to lead a team that includes a paediatrician, psychologists, behaviour therapists and the odd speech pathologist and occupational therapist. I see my patients in the limited hours of my daughter's kinder, which adds up to twelve hours a week. My evenings and weekends are often spent in front of the computer if I'm not in bed exhausted. Not very glamorous!

Along the way I have learnt a bucket load of valuable lessons that would probably be obvious to some, but they're lessons I've learnt the hard way!

Happiness is paramount

That tightrope I teeter on top of involves balancing giving what I've got to the various domains of my life. If what I'm giving isn't enough for some people – professionally or personally – then perhaps they don't have a place in my life. I find my balancing act is about knowing when to say 'no' and deciding how much I'm going to give of myself to others. Improving my personal boundaries and understanding what's my problem and what's not my problem has been essential.

I'm always dropping the ball

I've become used to the guilt associated with pretty much always not doing enough. (See above point! Sometimes the trade-off of saying no is letting people down.) There's always someone in the workplace I'm not supporting enough, family or friends I'm not seeing enough, and of course there's my child, who I'll always feel I'm not doing enough for. My success on any given day in any given area will most likely come at a cost in another area of my life. I accept this, though, and am able to accept that I don't need to be perfect.

People will judge
Controversially, I am sometimes that mum at the playground on my phone. My answer to those who judge – I am bloody lucky to be able to run a successful company that not only provides jobs but services the community. I get to drop my daughter off and pick her up from kinder most days. I can be involved in school life. And I can spend her days off from kinder with her and enjoying our time together. If the trade-off means that sometimes when we are together and my daughter is enjoying her independence, I'm taking a call from a doctor or emailing a parent in crisis, then so be it.

There are some inspirational people out there
One of the best parts of my job is that on a daily basis I hear the most inspirational stories from the most incredible parents out there. There are people who give up careers to raise their children with special needs. There are people who are grieving the most horrendous losses while getting on with life, and who can still smile and have a joke with you. **These people could be any of us and meeting them is a privilege and one of the reasons I continue to work in my profession.** To be honest, every parent who walks through my door and places their trust in me to help them is an inspiration. The honesty I encounter daily makes me feel honoured.

There are some really nasty people out there too …
Some people will try to shoot you down. I won't dwell on the negative, but I've had my fair share of encounters with toxic people. My solution – I do whatever I can to get them out of my

life. I don't need the negativity. These people don't get to me; I feel sorry for them and hope someone out there can help them see reason. Interestingly, each encounter I've had with these types of toxic people has taught me various valuable lessons.

Know when to say 'yes'

I've had incredible opportunities thrown my way, and I've learnt you can't say yes to them all. I am discerning about who I let into my world and which opportunities are worth my time and energy. I always come back to this: if I'm going to spend time away from my family, it had better be worth it. Yes, sometimes I have FOMO (fear of missing out) and haven't made the best decisions based on that! But in general, it comes down to weighing up the cost of the opportunity, whether that be time, effort, money or some other type of sacrifice.

Remember why you're doing it

I've been ready to throw in the towel a few times. I've had a handful of experiences while working for myself that have been extremely stressful. These have been across both the professional and business side of things, and neither is easier to manage. What has helped? I remember why I'm doing it. I make a choice each day to keep my business going. I could easily go and get a job working for someone else but I don't. Why? Because despite my 'hourly rate' probably being below the minimum wage, I enjoy my work. I enjoy the non-financial benefits that come with owning my own business and being able to support the community in my own way. I'm not restricted by red tape or other people's ideals and can follow my passions as they change.

Outsourcing

I outsource. Everything. When my business first picked up, I remember taking an afternoon off each week (of the three days I worked) to clean my house. But I soon realised that my time was better spent in the office. I also outsource a lot in business, because I'm trained as a psychologist. Not a lawyer, HR consultant, photocopier repairer or IT guru. I also believe in getting a bit of help from a psychologist to preserve mental health or to fill my knowledge gaps regarding stress management or anything else that needs addressing.

Be like Elsa and *Let It Go*

I've had to learn to practise what I preach to my patients and be cognitively flexible, and not give in to my anxious ways of running my life. Through lack of time and energy and the need to prioritise, I've had to forgo the control a bit. What does this look like? The crumbs under the dining table, the pile of washing on the spare bed, babysitters, frozen meals, delayed email responses, missed opportunities. Again, it comes back to priorities and figuring out what's important.

Perspective

I use an analogy with the families I work with. It's called 'eggs in baskets'. I literally draw a heap of circles (representing baskets) on a page and label them Family, Friends, Marriage, Self-care, Work, Health, Fun, etc. I then get the patient to draw their idea of how many 'eggs' are in each basket, which is determined by how much time and energy they devote to that particular domain of their life. Invariably, we find that the Work basket tends to be really full, to the detriment of the other life domains. This gives an opportunity for perspective, a wake-up call if you will.

The problem with having all our eggs in one or two baskets is that when something goes wrong in that area of our life, we lose perspective and it becomes a big deal. For instance, a family I was recently working with had all the eggs in the Work and Kids baskets. When the dad lost his job and struggled to be re-employed, he sank into a deep depression. Because he hadn't fostered any of the eggs in the Friends, Health and Fun baskets, he didn't have anyone or anything to fall back on, occupy him or support him. Take-home message – have a few eggs in all your baskets. At least then when you have a falling out with a friend, work becomes stressful, you injure yourself or your marriage hits a rough patch, you will have perspective and other parts of your life to draw happiness from.

I did it my way

Yeah, like Frank Sinatra, I do things my way. Must be the South African in me! Whether it's how I practise as a psychologist or how I run my business, I do it in a way that feels most comfortable for me. After all, I'm the one who needs to be able to sleep at night in response to the decisions I make. I've always been a very transparent person, and from the outset of my business I made a vow to 'keep it real' in business. I don't do gimmicks or sleazy networking. I do what I do in the best capacity I can, and I think I'm a good person. Of course, people will take advantage, and that's okay.

Decision fatigue is a thing

Apparently our ability to make 'good' decisions deteriorates over time when we are making a lot of decisions, particularly when both options to consider in the decision-making process have trade-offs (each option has both a negative and positive element). For working mums, I think this is totally why we might be more inclined to say 'yes' to the McDonald's drive-through on the way home from swimming at 5.30 on a Thursday night, because by this point in the day and week we are mentally depleted. Weighing up the pros and cons of the drive-through becomes exhausting. Apparently, I can also blame my impulse purchases on decision fatigue, so I'm getting behind this fancy concept.

Learn from the mistakes
I've made heaps. The people closest to me are probably in disbelief sometimes that, as a psychologist and business owner who appears so successful, I can make such bad decisions or monumental mistakes! But alas I do. Luckily, I'm a bit of a positive thinker, so I will always learn from mistakes. I encourage others to do the same.

So there they are. The lessons I've learnt. But what does it all mean? It is what it is. Making it fun has been essential for me – I wouldn't put myself through the stress if I didn't love what I do, and getting out of bed each day wasn't something I looked forward to. And quickly deciphering those who are willing to be remotely interested in my life and support me in my endeavours allows me to invest the time and energy in relationships that matter. The things I am grateful for, either with or without the hashtag, are the people who support me and believe in me. Like all working mums, without my support team, I couldn't enjoy both the working and the 'mumming' as much as I do.

Know that happiness is paramount, so allow yourself to say 'no' when you need to. Remember why you're doing what you're doing. You can only do your best, so invest your time and energy into the things that matter most to you and give yourself permission to let some things go. And if you need help to do that, don't be afraid to seek help from a psychologist or speak to your doctor.

26

Ella

Making a difference and running for parliament

Ella Haddad is a health services advocate who is an endorsed candidate for the Tasmanian Labor Party at the next state election. Ella has held positions on the boards of TasCOSS, Women's Health Tasmania and the Tasmanian Council for AIDS, Hepatitis and Related Diseases.

I was born in Melbourne in the late 1970s, to a Lebanese migrant father and a mum who grew up on a Victorian dairy farm. My family was pretty standard for Melbourne, even in those days. First-generation Australian on one side, sixth on the other.

But when we moved to Hobart in the mid-1980s, I was somewhat of an ethnic novelty. While Hobart was familiar with waves of Western European migrants and several Greek and Italian families, Lebanese was less familiar. I am deeply proud of my heritage, but as a young person who did not like to be singled out or sat in the spotlight, this attention felt uncomfortable and unwanted.

It's been great to see Hobart change and become more multicultural in the last thirty years. But that feeling I got as a young child of noticing and celebrating difference has not left me.

I learnt from a young age that everyone counts. That everyone has a story to tell and should be listened to and treated with respect. In my family, I learnt that difference is something to be celebrated, not something that should divide us.

My parents taught me to always have a healthy questioning of authority. Not a disrespect, but simply to always ask myself and encourage others to ask: what is right and what can I do to make a difference?

It was in grade three that I decided to take a 'log of claims' to my primary school principal. While I can't recall the detail of the list, I remember going to my fellow students and asking them the things that concerned them most. There were things about the playground, the classroom and some examples of bullying or teasing that made the list. When the morning of my appointment with the principal came, I was terrified. I knew the things on my list had to be raised but in that moment, waiting to see him, I absolutely questioned why I had taken it upon myself to raise them! A bundle of nerves, I went into the office – sure I'd be told off or told I was 'too big for my boots'. But to my surprise, he listened and thanked me for raising the concerns.

Although it was, at that time, the most nerve-wracking experience I'd ever had, it enlivened in me something much bigger. A strong desire to make change, and a realisation that no matter how scared I felt, I had the capacity to represent others and make a positive difference.

Fast-forward to high school and university, and it may be no surprise that it was politics that took my interest. I joined the Australian Labor Party at seventeen and held positions within

Young Labor and the party. I was secretary of the student union at my university and a delegate to several National Union of Students conferences.

While on the student union and involved in Young Labor politics, I organised campaigns for things including stopping library closures at the uni, reducing tutorial class sizes, fighting for adequate levels of income support from the government for students, and reducing university HECS fees. Each of these campaigns was exciting, but every time I started out, I still felt myself in that bundle of nerves in the principal's office. Each time I stood in front of a conference to speak, or addressed a rally, there they were again – those nerves in the pit of my stomach. The desire to fight for what was right was still there, but so were the nerves!

My first professional job after finishing uni was as an electorate officer to a busy federal Labor MP. There I learnt firsthand the hardships many Tasmanians go through daily. Difficulties in accessing housing. Health treatment. Community services. Pensions. I saw how the 'system' can chew people up and spit them out and saw so many instances of people doing the right thing yet being treated the wrong way. I could see clearly there were better ways to do things. Better ways to treat people. Ways to improve the systems of government that are there to protect the most vulnerable in our communities.

I had my first daughter when I was quite young – 26 and not long out of uni. We didn't earn much and nine months was the longest we could afford for me to be out of the workforce. It was so hard leaving my daughter at nine months of age to go to childcare four days a week while I took up a new job working for MPs in the state parliament. I remember an older female colleague whose kids were grown, telling me in my first week back at work that she just could not believe that young mums like me were able to leave our kids. She said she recalled her years of staying at home with her children and not leaving them for even a few hours until they were toddlers. I knew she meant well, but of course all I could hear was that she thought she loved her kids more than I loved mine. Still breastfeeding and struggling to be away from my little one, the words hit hard!

What made it bearable was the work I got to do. I got to work on the Tasmanian Anti-discrimination Act, a law that protects all Tasmanians from discrimination on the grounds of gender, sexuality, race and so on. I got to work on the Relationships Act – a law that recognises same-sex couples including overseas marriage and an important stop-gap in protection of the rights of LGBTI families until marriage equality is finally achieved in Australia. I got to work on a community consultation for a Human Rights Act for Tasmania, something that would codify many of the rights we take for granted in Australia, but are in fact not protected by law.

Another shock was when another colleague suggested I should go and work elsewhere. Not because of the quality of my work, but because 'jobs in politics don't suit mums with young kids'. The shock was not the comment – we all know mums in the workplace are often thought less of. **The shock was that my husband had an identical job in the same organisation, was the same age as me and father to the same child – and yet nobody was suggesting he should find a job elsewhere or that**

a job in politics wasn't suitable for a young dad. The irony was not lost on either of us!

That experience started a steely resolve in me to prove them wrong. For good or for bad I stuck it out for four more years. My colleague was right: the job was not easy to juggle with kids, but it was worth it!

During the next five years I found myself as a single mum, juggling full-time work with two young kids and volunteer commitments on three community sector boards to top it all off. While they were challenging years, I truly learnt we can do so much. It was empowering to realise I could live on my own, care for my kids on my own, handle my finances alone, and take on new challenges, changing careers to work in the community and health sectors as well as taking up more study.

I know that's not everyone's experience and I am very lucky – it has been possible not only because I have worked hard at each job I have held, but also because I have had excellent bosses who have understood the pressures of single parenting – all parenting really! – and have been willing to take a chance on me, knowing I can do the work even if it means sometimes having to work from home with sick little ones or leave early to attend a parent–teacher evening. It was also only possible because I was lucky enough to have a supportive family: my mum, dad and sister – along with amazing fellow single mum friends who were all enormous supports to each other. And now with a wonderful new partner who is fantastically supportive to me and an amazing stepdad.

Now that I'm a manager of a small team, I am glad I can return this respect to my colleagues as they juggle their own life circumstances including young kids, elderly parents, study and health concerns.

So in my jobs, I have always tried to make a difference – and more recently, I've made another 'bundle of nerves' decision and nominated for state parliament.

The election campaign is in full swing. We don't know when the election will be called, but I am working as hard as I can to get my message out into the community about how I believe I can best make a positive difference next: that is, as a member of parliament, making good laws that will benefit Tasmanians.

I thought long and hard about running for parliament, for over ten years. So it was not a decision I took lightly. It's lovely to see how my nine-year-old daughter is pleased with my decision. When I explained to her that I was running for parliament, she responded that she was 'glad someone will beat Donald Trump' (I think the explanation on the differences between the US and Tasmanian political systems can come later – for now I'm just glad she's on the right track with her support!) As the new Leader of the Labor Party Rebecca White has said these jobs require sacrifice, but we do them because we care and we really want to make the place we live a better one.

The Tasmanian electoral system is a tricky one – and we have six Labor candidates vying for just a handful of seats in the electorate I'm running in. But that's not enough to stop me from taking the chance. I truly believe that if people start electing progressive, compassionate people to parliament, instead of those who are just in it for power or ego, things really will change and improve in politics in Tasmania.

The bundle of nerves may never go away. But sometimes that's the very thing that will push you that little bit further to achieve the best you can.

27

KATE

Taking a breath between the busyness

Kate Cashman from The Breath Between is a rest and renewal coach, academic, writer and speaker. With a background in legal academia and a PhD in evidence law and forensic criminology, she finds balance and passion in teaching, research, writing and coaching. As a coach and speaker, Kate uses her legal, management, research and coaching qualifications, together with her personal experience, to help inspire and support busy professionals and entrepreneurs to live more balanced and holistic lives.

Every day, the world will drag you by the hand, yelling, 'This is important! And this is important! And this is important! You need to worry about this! And this! And this!' And each day, it's up to you to yank your hand back, put it on your heart and say, 'No. This is what's important.'

— Iain Thomas

I began a journey of 'busyness' at the age of fourteen. I fell in love with school and everything about my time there. That meant I embraced all opportunities that came my way and although I was interested and engaged, I was also tired, my immune system struggled, and I didn't get enough sleep.

I spent my time playing sport, debating, public speaking, being on the school council and Prefect Board, competing in academic competitions, singing in the choir and playing flute in the concert band. I was never pushed to be involved like that – it was always an internal drive and pressure that I put on myself to take advantage of anything that was interesting or that took me beyond my comfort zone. I just never really learnt how to have an 'off switch'.

Little did I know that I was learning how to fill my time exhaustively and starting what would become a fifteen-year journey of busyness. I slowly forgot to take time to daydream, kick around with my friends doing nothing and embrace life at a slower pace. School reports read, 'Kate will go far, but she burns the candle at both ends.'

The speed stayed with me throughout university. I launched myself into a combined business and law degree, and again became involved in everything on offer. Those five years were characterised by intense periods of study, part-time work and then travel each summer using my scholarship to try to feel like myself again. Ready to rinse and repeat the same thing all over again the following year.

I always knew there was a more balanced life for me somewhere, but it took me a number of years to get the point where it was something my body and soul needed in a big way.

There were times when I had glimpses of that life, though. The year after I graduated with a First Class Honours degree in law and business, my (now) husband and I spent the year in Africa. We started in Kenya and bought a 1983 beige Landcruiser that we fondly named 'Helga'. She was our beloved home for the better part of eight months and we travelled through eastern and southern Africa, falling in love with the continent and its people.

Balance, for that year, meant embracing life on the road in a tent too small for both of us, learning to use a high-lift jack while surrounded by elephants and giraffes (I can tell you, it happened quickly!), and spending a significant amount of time volunteering our time to help in children's homes and primary schools.

Working with a small children's centre in the Ngong Hills outside of Nairobi, and later building a primary school room in Ruhunga, not far from the gorillas of Bwindi National Park in Uganda, were my two main projects. Far from an organised 'volunteer holiday', the time with the children at both of these amazing places was transformative. I felt blessed to have spent time with these people in these places, and the kids and I relished our adventures together in the surrounding hills. Life was relatively simple, uncluttered and magical. I realised that although volunteering was a way to help make others' lives better, it shifted the focus away from me for a while and meant I could be productive without being busy. It felt expansive and I knew that my life was changed.

I came back from Africa and resigned from my graduate corporate law job three weeks before I was due to move to Melbourne. After being on the road with fresh air on my face for almost a year, the thought of being in a suit on level 37 of a Melbourne high rise just didn't appeal any more. It was the ideal life for many that I knew, and they loved it, but I knew in my heart that it wasn't for me. I was scared senseless. I'd missed job applications in Tasmania and for the first time in a long time, I had no idea what was to come next.

After a month or so of being home in Tasmania, I took up the offer of a scholarship to study a PhD in forensic criminology and evidence law, looking at how lawyers use and understand DNA evidence in criminal trials. It was a passion-filled project and one that allowed me to explore a love of research, teaching, travel and academic life more generally. It also opened up a new and flexible way of working, and one that meant I could focus on starting my family and having children of my own.

I had a lot of people telling me that having children during postgraduate study was a great idea. The flexibility of working from home and time with my small children meant that I could work on my writing late at night, or in the wee hours of the morning, depending on when I was most productive. But I also had people telling me that there was no way I could string a sentence together after sleep deprivation and baby brain would take over my life. The truth was perhaps somewhere in the middle.

My first baby was a sleeper. He had his moments, but he slept fairly predictably of his own accord, and it meant I could quietly read and summarise journal articles and write drafts of papers and stories. At the time, I thought these words made sense. When I revisited them, closer to submission, it was obvious that they would need a little more work. But they were written words, and that made them productive in some small way.

It was true that I was home for all the best moments in that first eighteen months. It was also true that baby brain, to some extent, took over some days – and even some weeks.

I took time away from teaching and returned to my research and teaching part-time as my son spent time with my husband and my mother for a day each week.

However, even with the benefits of a flexible workspace and hours, I found balance at home hard. I had always used travel to feel more rested and renewed, and here I was with a mortgage on a flat (and later a house), married, with my first beautiful child and finishing a PhD part-time. Long-term travel would be a few years off, and I had to focus on modelling the life I wanted for our family. Even with the flexibility of academic life and postgraduate research, I still only knew how to live a 'busy' life. I became restless.

A small car accident on the way to the Supreme Court one day to assess students for a mock trial signalled that my body felt restless again, too. I felt as if I was having a heart attack. I couldn't breathe properly and my chest felt as if it had been split in two. But this wasn't the first time I'd felt uncomfortable with my breathing.

Each time I said yes to too many people and took on too many projects, at one point or another my breathing would become shallow and my chest would begin to hurt. Five X-rays on, any physiological reasons were ruled out. I didn't know about situational anxiety back then – but I do now. A physiological presentation for what was a mental, spiritual and emotional overload. The busyness had found a way to make me feel unwell.

It's been three years since I ran my car off the road that night. I've spent that time embracing the quiet and focusing on balance over busy in small amounts. I had to re-learn who I was and what I truly wanted for myself and my family.

In the quiet, I felt reassured that I had the power, the persistence, the passion and the patience to create a life that I loved and didn't feel I needed to escape from in order to feel rested and renewed. But I was so accustomed to the 'noise' from my research, family, a social life and balancing voluntary and paid work that it was a slow process. But my goodness, was it a worthwhile one.

I resigned from committees that didn't align with the mission and vision I had created for myself. I read books for enjoyment again. I rediscovered regular meditation, even if it was for fifteen minutes before the house woke. I had my second child and I was again home with her for the best bits. I gave myself permission to rest into that time. I still loved my academic work, but I only said yes to projects that challenged me and that I was passionate about.

I realised not long after my second child was born that there were parts of myself I wanted to explore more, and it wasn't happening in my life at that point. I was passionate both about helping others and the process I had been through in slowing down and saying no to being busy. I knew there would be others on the same road as me. I took a leap of faith, and before I went back to teaching I did a coaching course to learn how to translate that passion into practice. Giving myself that permission created an infinitely powerful shift. I wasn't just 'academic' Kate, or 'mother' Kate or 'wife' Kate. Those roles were all so important, but they weren't everything and I wanted more. I leaned into creating my own coaching business and began working with busy people who felt the same pull to slow down and feel more rested and renewed by their life like I had, but who needed support and encouragement to take those important first steps. My business, The Breath Between, was born.

Until that point I had continued to volunteer my time to organisations, committees and boards. My time in Africa taught me just how incredible this felt and the changes I could make to the world and those around me. When the time came to be more balanced and embrace a sense of renewal in this part of my life, too, I focused on two organisations in particular.

The first was the Child Health Association of Tasmania. Supporting young families in my home state was and still is one of my top priorities, particularly as the mother of small children myself. The second was a relatively new organisation called Insight Mindfulness Education (IME). Created in Tasmania by a local teacher, Grant Milbourne, IME facilitates mindfulness and meditation retreats for teenagers in Australia to learn more about themselves and these amazing practices to support their own wellbeing. I knew that my inability to say no for so many years began in those teenage years, and part of my commitment to creating a renewal revolution in my business and life now includes supporting teenagers to give themselves that gift in those early years.

My PhD was finished in the year after that shift. Funny, that. I feel like it could have been done a year earlier, but two babies, lots of travel and taking time with my family meant that I didn't want to rush that work. I didn't want to rush life and parenthood.

Volunteer work, my coaching business – they're all equally valid, important and expansive roles that I play. I wanted to enjoy my family, my relationship, my friends and my own life, without feeling like life starts when I finish the next 'big thing'. And so it was with my research as well. When I gave myself permission to have a passion-filled life, the balance came. I became a more confident and empowered mother and a purpose-driven woman.

I'll admit, though, that old habits die hard. The pull to be 'busy' is always there for me. The mother guilt – that I shouldn't be focusing on my own life and passions, and instead I should throw everything I have towards my children – well, it's what society sometimes still expects. Hours worked is often our social currency and a personal drive to succeed is often hard to juggle with self-imposed 'balance'.

But each day, I step toward balance, embrace rest and renewal, and give myself permission to choose that, and to show my children how important that time really is.

Travel is no longer about escaping the busy only to return to it after my adventures are over. Travel is about the joy, the adventure, the knowledge and the connection with myself, my family and those I meet along the way.

Because I've embraced a renewal revolution, from home.

Schedule time for 'white space' – nothing planned, nothing else organised, just total freedom to do with what you wish. This time is entirely for you – to allow you to feel rested, or perhaps full of energy, but certainly, in some way, full of joy. It may be five minutes here and there, an hour or two, or half a day. But relish the time you can choose to sit, lie down, read or just stare at the clouds. You will not only feel more like 'yourself' again, but you will be a better mother, with more energy to give others.

The women whom I love and admire for their strength and grace did not get that way because shit worked out. They got that way because shit went wrong, and they handled it. They handled it in a thousand different ways on a thousand different days, but they handled it.

– Elizabeth Gilbert

What we wish we could have also covered

When writing and collaborating with our amazing contributors, we struggled a little with the reality that although we hoped this book would help as many of our fellow working parents as possible, we simply couldn't cover every situation parents might face.

This includes, of course, acknowledging that fathers are also balancing paid work with parenthood. In no way do we wish to perpetuate the myth that it should only be mothers who should be worrying about how to balance paid work and raising children. It most certainly should not! But as working mums ourselves, we felt it most natural to start with the stories of the amazing women around us.

We acknowledge that everyone has a story, and we're incredibly inspired by the brave women who have shared theirs, in the hope of helping others.

Thank you.

– Danielle and Louise

Finding out more

If you'd like to know more about the activities, businesses and passions of the women in this book, please see the list below.

Alisa Camplin
www.alisacamplin.com
www.finnansgift.com
Finnan's Gift helps save and improve lives by providing tangible gifts to the Royal Children's Hospital, Melbourne. Whether it be a piece of critical equipment, much-needed research, advanced training or greater support for patients and families, Finnan's Gift makes a difference while raising awareness of Congenital Heart Disease.

Annie Nolan
www.uncannyannie.com.au
www.pramjam.org.au
The Pram Jam helps raise awareness and funds to help prevent stillbirth and complications from babies being born prematurely. All mothers, fathers, grandparents, family and friends are invited to grab a pram and pound the pavement in this annual fundraising initiative to help bring mums and bubs home safely.

George McEncroe
www.shebah.com.au
Australia's first all-female rideshare service, Shebah, donates 1 per cent of all fares to charity. The list of charities is a living

one, and at the time of writing includes charities that help women experiencing homelessness, help young people learn about respectful relationships, and help people struggling with anxiety and depression after the birth of a child.

Missy Higgins
www.missyhiggins.com
https://350.org.au
350.org Australia is a not-for-profit project that aims to rapidly end fossil fuels by building a global climate movement. The number 350 means climate safety: to preserve a liveable planet, scientists tell us we must reduce the amount of CO_2 in the atmosphere from its current level of 413 parts per million (ppm) to below 350 ppm.

Aleisha Rasheed
www.altonaacupuncture.com

Amanda Abel
http://www.centreforchilddevelopment.com/

Carly Naughton
https://perilsofapassableparent.wordpress.com/

Chloe Chant
http://www.mystory.nsw.edu.au/

Christine Jolly
www.cradle2kindy.com.au

Danielle Ross Walls
www.daniellerosswalls.com

Ella Haddad
www.facebook.com/EllaHaddadMP

Irene Falcone
www.nourishedlife.com.au

Jade McKenzie
www.eventhead.com.au

Jade Wisely
www.jadewisely.com

Jen Murnaghan
www.digitaldandy.com.au

Jenny Weber
www.bobbrown.org.au

Jessica Sjöhage
Instagram: @swaussiemum

Kate Cashman
www.katecashman.com

Kristy Vallely
www.theimperfectmum.com.au

Maria Smith
www.bounceaustralia.com
www.myalura.com.au

Mel Butel
www.playact.com.au

Louise Correcha
www.hummingbirdwriting.com

Rhiannon Colarossi
www.wellbeingweb.com.au

Helpful resources

The following national organisations can provide assistance or advice to working parents, either for free or at a low cost. In some instances, they can direct you to local assistance. It is not an all-inclusive list, but may be of some help.

Kindly note that we list these resources with the best of intentions as a point from which to start for advice, but we are not responsible for any individual advice given.

Australian resources

Australian Breastfeeding Association
www.breastfeeding.asn.au

Bereavement Information and Referral Service
www.grief.org.au

Beyond Blue: depression, anxiety and mental health
www.beyondblue.org.au

Emergency services: police, fire and ambulance
Dial 000

Fair Work Ombudsman: Australian Government
www.fairwork.gov.au

Department of Human Services
www.humanservices.gov.au
www.1800respect.org.au

Lifeline Australia: crisis support and suicide prevention
www.lifeline.org.au

MensLine Australia: men's health and support
https://mensline.org.au

Parentline Services: parenting advice and counselling
https://kidshelpline.com.au/parents/parentline-services

Perinatal Anxiety and Depression Australia (PANDA)
www.panda.org.au

Relationships Australia
www.relationships.org.au

National Sexual Assault, Domestic and Family Violence Counselling Service
www.1800respect.org.au

Support for working parents
supportingworkingparents.humanrights.gov.au/employees/working-parents-quick-guide-your-rights

Women's Legal Services Australia
www.wlsa.org.au

Women's Information Referral Exchange (WIRE)
www.wire.org.au

New Zealand resources

Emergency services: police, fire, ambulance and civil defence
Dial 111

Employment New Zealand
https://www.employment.govt.nz

Family Violence: It's not OK
www.areyouok.org.nz/family-violence

Government website for parents: Information about education for parents and carers.
https://parents.education.govt.nz

Lifeline Aotearoa: crisis support and suicide prevention
https://www.lifeline.org.nz

Mental Health Foundation of New Zealand (includes crisis line)
https://www.mentalhealth.org.nz

Mothers Helpers: antenatal and postnatal depression and anxiety support
https://www.mothershelpers.co.nz

New Zealand Breastfeeding Alliance (NZBA)
https://www.babyfriendly.org.nz

Parent Help
Free parent helpline: 0800 568 856
www.parenthelp.org.nz

Plunket: The largest provider of free support services for the development, health and wellbeing of children under five in New Zealand.
http://www.plunket.org.nz

Sands: pregnancy, baby and infant loss support
www.sands.org.nz

The Parenting Place: courses, events and resources for parents
https://www.theparentingplace.com

Women's Refuge: legal advice and other issues facing women
https://www.womensrefuge.org.nz

Acknowledgements

To our inspiring and brave contributors – our heartfelt gratitude for sharing your stories to help other parents.

Thank you also to Rex, Sam, Sonya, Sarah and Karen at Finch – then Lucy and Jason at Fontaine – for your invaluable knowledge and guidance.

From Danielle

For my beautiful boys Liam and Fraser – I hope that you one day find work that lights you up.

To Dave, my parents, family and dear friends – thank you for your support and for sharing the excitement of this journey.

To Louise, thank you. What a great team we make. Working with you is a joy.

From Louise

For my daughter and muse Sophie Helena. In whatever you do, may you always be led by the same strong, wise voice that you have used to unequivocally announce yourself to the world since the moment you were born (and, I suspect, even before). May you also keep telling people who call you a princess that you are, in fact, a queen.

To Julian, my great friends and my Australian, Colombian and Czech families – thank you, *gracias, děkuji*.

To Danielle, the professional yin to my yang. Thank you so, so much.

www.ingramcontent.com/pod-product-compliance
Lightning Source LLC
Chambersburg PA
CBHW032107090426
42743CB00007B/267

9781922409119